Bahamas

Berlitz Publishing Company, Inc.

Princeton   Mexico City   Dublin   Eschborn   Singapore

Text:	revised by Lindsay Bennett; original text by Don Larrimore
Editor:	Christopher Billy
Photography:	Pete Bennett except pages 69, 70, 72, 74, 92, 93 (Daniel Vittet)
Cover Photo:	Pete Bennett
Photo Editor:	Naomi Zinn
Layout:	Media Content Marketing, Inc.
Cartography:	Ortelius Design

Although the publisher tries to insure the accuracy of all the information in this book, changes are inevitable and errors may result. The publisher cannot be responsible for any resulting loss, inconvenience, or injury. If you find an error in this guide, please let the editors know by writing to Berlitz Publishing Company, 400 Alexander Park, Princeton, NJ 08540-6306.

ISBN 2-8315-7212-6
Revised 1999 – First Printing October 1999

Printed in Italy
019/907 REV

Bahamas

THE BAHAMAS AND THE BAHAMIANS

Like a handful of emeralds scattered across blue velvet, the verdant islands of the Commonwealth of the Bahamas stretch across 100,000 sq miles (259,000 sq km) of the Atlantic Ocean. The 700 islands and numerous smaller cays (pronounced "keys") that comprise this semitropical archipelago start 55 miles (90 km) east of Palm Beach, Florida, and arc 600 miles (970 km) southeast toward eastern Cuba and Haiti, like a series of stepping stones linking North America with the Caribbean.

Some of the islands are only a few hundred square meters in size, but together they make up an area of 5,380 sq miles (14,000 sq km), slightly smaller than the area of the Hawaiian Islands. Only 100 of the islands are inhabited; many of these have become private playgrounds for the rich and super-rich. Even fewer—37 to be exact—have settlements or towns. This leaves many hundreds of cays that are totally natural, untouched by the destructive influence of humans and offering pristine habitats to hundreds of bird and animal species.

The Bahamas islands are the flattened peaks of a huge ancient mountain range that once towered many thousands of feet into the sky. They now lie low in the water, the highest point—Mount Alvernia on Cat Island—being only 206 ft (65 m) above sea level. The eastern coastlines of the islands break the long tidal fetch that travels across the Atlantic; on the sheltered western coastline, coral outcrops have produced vast shallow sand banks that reflect waters of myriad translucent blues and greens.

Indeed, it was these characteristic shallow banks that gave the Bahamas islands their name. When Spanish explorers

A uniformed policeman keeps his eye on the goings-on in bustling Nassau.

came to map the area in the 16th century, they named the area *baja mar,* or shallow seas, as a warning to the galleons that would be sailing through the waters. The name was later anglicized and the Bahamas were born.

The warning on Spanish maps unfortunately did little to stop ships from running aground or foundering on the treacherous shoals; even today treasure lost centuries ago is still being discovered and salvaged.

The islands of the Bahamas were claimed by the English, but hundreds of secret coves became home to pirates and smugglers who turned their backs on nationality to enter the brotherhood of buccaneers. They ruled the seas, plundering ships at will, and then spent their ill-gotten gains in the bars and brothels of Nassau town, the main settlement.

Later, as the English colonies of North America fought for independence, the islands became a refuge for fleeing loyalists who sought to make a new life on these remote, picturesque cays. Cotton production brought a number of slaves to the islands, but the crops proved to be poor and depleted the already weak soil. Sponge gathering was devastated after a fungus attacked the crop, and sisal was produced more cheaply in South America. The population eked out a living, but little more than that. Things changed in the 1920s, however, when the Bahamas profited from the American policy of Prohibition. Rum-running became a major industry, and well-to-do Americans began making the short trip to the Bahamas to be able to drink legally, and to indulge in other pleasures.

Since World War II, the Bahamas has worked hard to extend the service it provided during Prohibition and has turned itself into a "paradise" for holiday-makers. The dazzling beaches are covered with fine sand that ranges from bright white to pastel pink. The sun shines year-round, with temperatures ranging from the high 60s to the high 80s fahrenheit. To these natural

Sea treasure: the ubiquitous conch, touted as the Bahamian aphrodisiac, is a delicious staple of the island diet.

ingredients have been added just about every amenity and service needed for the perfect holiday. Everything centers on New Providence, where most of the tourists stay and half of the Bahamian population lives. One of the largest cruise ports in the world, Nassau can accommodate 15 large ships at one time. English "pomp," stout forts, and colonial houses attract history buffs. Grand Bahama, the second most populous island, has Freeport–Lucaya, Nassau's younger, less genteel "American" cousin; nightlife here is more lavish and audacious than in Nassau. Both islands have large resort hotels that offer watersports, floor shows, and casinos where you can enjoy the thrill of winning or the dejection of losing. Golf courses entice you to lower your handicap. Tour buses plow a path around the attractions, and duty-free shops tempt you to buy that little luxury item you've been denying yourself for so long. Hundreds of day-trippers cruise to both islands, eager to do it all before they have to get back on the boat.

On the smaller and more remote islands—called the Out Islands or Family Islands—intimate resorts cater to your every need and make it possible for you to forget about schedules, deadlines, and traffic jams. The most difficult decision you'll have to make is what to pick from the extensive dinner menu. While the clubs and casinos may not play on into the night, during the day you'll be worn out by walks along the beach and other strenuous activities, such as collecting sea shells, enjoying long lunches, and applying sunblock. The whole trip could prove to be exhausting!

The lure of the Bahamas is, of course, as much about the sea as it is about the land. The waters of the western Atlantic are still some of the clearest and most beautiful in the world. In summer the shallows are glassy still and range from azure blue to emerald green; the deep ocean channels reflect a deep blue that can best be appreciated from the air.

The sandy shallows are ideal for swimming and snorkeling, and since the development of scuba (an acronym for **s**elf-**c**ontained **u**nderwater **b**reathing **a**pparatus) gear in the 1930s, the seas around the Bahamas have become a top destination for diving enthusiasts from around the world.

The waters of the Bahamas support a vast range of life and contain 5 percent of the world's coral. Diving around the reef surfaces and the vertical reef walls is complemented by many ship wrecks and artificial sites—large, concrete blocks which are placed on the sea bed to encourage coral growth—surrounding the islands.

Yachtsmen up the mast in Port Lucaya, a popular marina.

Fish species mass in the vast shallows along with urchins and starfish. Yet deep ocean channels cut between some island groups—the Tongue of the Ocean between Andros and New Providence, for example, is 6,000 ft (2,000 m) deep—and these provide a thoroughfare for a number of large fish and marine mammal species, such as sharks, rays, dolphins, and turtles.

This not only provides excitement for divers, who can watch shark feeding in the wild on some Bahamian islands, but also to fishermen. The vast numbers of large fish species, including record breaking marlin and bonefish, make for some of the most challenging and thrilling sport-fishing in the world.

On top of the water, the shallow channels and sheltered seas provide ideal waters for sailing and cruising. Hundreds of unmanned cays offer idyllic destinations and mooring points. The desert island you always dreamed about is somewhere in the Bahamas—the Exumas themselves have one cay for every day of year, and that is only one part of the vast Commonwealth. Many lie only a few hours sailing time from the hubbub of Nassau.

The Bahamian people are among the friendliest you'll ever meet, and they are eager to share the homeland they love with visitors. The population is a fascinating mixture of descendants

of the Loyalist settlers who left America after the American Revolution, freedom lovers who escaped religious persecution, and ex-slaves set free following emancipation. This mixture, which could have produced a society fraught with problems, has evolved into a gentle, sociable, and happy people, proud of their homeland and the progress they have made since independence in 1973. With a stable economy,

Like riding a bicycle, you'll never forget picturesque Harbour Island, Eleuthera.

good health, and no taxes, it's no wonder that a smile comes naturally to all Bahamians. All the communities still have strong religious faith, the pretty churches are full on Sundays, and a conversation about some future event always ends with "…God willing" or "…with the Lord's blessing."

To make the most of your trip you'll need to tune your mind to "Bahamian time." On New Providence and Grand Bahama this may not be much slower than at home, but on the Out Islands, time definitely runs more slowly, and nothing is so important that it can't wait a while. People are more important than to-do lists, so a leisurely exchange of greet-

The perfect souvenir…A local craftswoman shows off her straw wares in Andros.

ings and an inquiry about your family's well-being precedes any business activity. This genuine thoughtfulness also extends to visitors; someone will always go out of their way to be helpful, in ways that have been lost in more developed locations.

Every island has its own individual character, forged by a unique history and development, in fact the Bahamas could be said to be several different holiday experiences in one country, so it's important to choose your island carefully to get the kind of holiday you want.

A BRIEF HISTORY

Centuries before the arrival of Columbus, a peaceful Amerindian people who called themselves the *Luccucairi* had settled in the Bahamas. Originally from South America, they had traveled up through the Caribbean islands, surviving by cultivating modest crops and from what they caught from sea and shore. Nothing in the experience of these gentle people could have prepared them for the arrival of the *Pinta,* the *Niña,* and the *Santa Maria* at San Salvador on 12 October 1492. Columbus believed that he had reached the East Indies and mistakenly called these people Indians. We know them today as the Lucayans. Columbus claimed the island and others in the Bahamas for his royal Spanish patrons, but not finding the gold and other riches he was seeking, he stayed for only two weeks before sailing towards Cuba.

The Spaniards never bothered to settle in the Bahamas, but the number of shipwrecks attest that their galleons frequently passed through the archipelago en route to and from the Caribbean, Florida, Bermuda, and their home ports. On Eleuthera the explorers dug a fresh-water well—at a spot now known as "Spanish Wells"—which was used to replenish the supplies of water on their ships before they began the long journey back to Europe with their cargoes of South American gold. As for the Lucayans, within 25 years all of them, perhaps some 30,000 people, were removed from the Bahamas to work—and die—in Spanish gold mines and on farms and pearl fisheries on Hispaniola (Haiti), Cuba, and elsewhere in the Caribbean.

English sea captains also came to know the beautiful but deserted Bahamian islands during the 17th century. England's first formal move was on 30 October 1629, when Charles I granted the Bahamas and a chunk of the American

A plaque commemorates Columbus's historic 1492 landing, San Salvador.

south to his Attorney General, Sir Robert Health. But nothing came of that, nor of a rival French move in 1633 when Cardinal Richelieu, the 17th-century French statesman, tried claiming the islands for France.

Colonization and Piracy

In 1648 a group of English Puritans from Bermuda, led by William Sayle, sailed to Bahamian waters and established the first permanent European settlement on the island they named Eleutheria (now Eleuthera) after the Greek word for freedom. The 70 colonists called themselves the Eleutherian Adventurers, but life was very difficult and the colony never flourished, though Sayle was long honored for the effort. In 1666 a small-

Slow down—you're on "island time." Sleepy Gregory Town, Eleuthera, makes an ideal getaway.

er island (called Sayle's island) with a fine harbor was settled by Bermudians and renamed New Providence. It was later to become known as Nassau, capital of the Bahamas.

In 1670 six Lords Proprietors of Carolina were granted the Bahama islands by Charles II, but for nearly 50 years their weak governors on New Providence either couldn't or wouldn't suppress the piracy raging through the archipelago. Then, in 1684, to avenge countless raids against their ships, the Spanish dispatched a powerful squadron from Cuba to attack Nassau. This sent the majority of the English settlers fleeing to Jamaica or Massachusetts, but didn't have much effect on the pirates.

Most feared of the 1,000 or more swashbucklers operating from the New Providence lair was Edward Teach, better known as Blackbeard. Today you can visit a tower east of Nassau named after him. Another two infamous pirates were women: Anne Bonney and Mary Read had exceptionally bloodthirsty reputations and are still celebrated in the Bahamas. The pirates raided anything on the sea, living totally lawless—and often not very lengthy—lives. Moreover, there was not always a clear distinction between pirates and privateers, the latter officially authorized by their governments to plunder enemy ships during time of war. Anarchy and confusion reigned throughout the area.

In 1718, shortly after the Bahamas became a crown colony, Captain Woodes Rogers, a renowned ex-privateer, was named the first royal governor. Arriving in Nassau with a powerful force and promising amnesty for surrender, he became a legend by cleaning out many of the pirates and establishing some order. This incident inspired the national motto *Expulsis Piratis—Restituta Commercia* (Pirates Expelled—Commerce Restored), which was retained until 1971.

A few years later Rogers quit the islands only to return for a second time in 1729 after a period of bankruptcy and debtor's prison in England. Before he died in Nassau in 1732 he had summoned the Bahamas' first official Assembly, composed of 16 elected members for New Providence and four each for Harbour Island and Eleuthera. At this time, in all the Bahamas there were only about 2,000 settlers.

New Providence knew some spells of prosperity in the mid-18th century as privateering resumed with England at war with Spain. The town of Nassau expanded, and improvements were made between 1760 and 1768 by another revered governor, William Shirley from Massachusetts.

The American Revolutionary War

When the 13 American colonies, enraged by the Stamp Tax, got into the war that eventually brought independence, the Bahamas somewhat reluctantly found itself on England's side. But reluctance dissolved as profits from privateering once again flowed into Nassau. This time the plundered vessels were American, but not all the victories were won by the privateers. On 3 March 1776, a rebel squadron under Commodore Esek Hopkins arrived and occupied Nassau for two weeks, a bloodless undertaking that emptied the island's forts of arms and other military supplies. A smaller and equally non-violent American operation against the town in January 1778 lasted less than three days.

As the colonies' war effort picked up steam, both France and Spain weighed in against the British. In May 1782, New Providence surrendered to a large Spanish-American invasion fleet from Cuba and for the next year a Spanish governor ruled the Bahamas.

News traveled slowly in those days. The Treaty of Versailles in 1783 formally restored the Bahamas to the British, but actual liberation came through a famous escapade that would never have happened in the age of the telegraph. Lieutenant-Colonel Andrew Deveaux, a loyalist from South Carolina, sailed from Florida with six ships, picked up men and fishing boats at Harbour Island and Eleuthera, and "invaded" Nassau. Though vastly outnumbered and outgunned, Deveaux employed elaborate ruses with his little boats to convince the Spanish defenders that his force was overpowering. The humiliating Spanish surrender is proudly recalled in Bahamian history, even though it was all unnecessary: the peace treaty had been signed the previous week.

Deveaux was the first of some 7,000 loyalists who, with slaves and the promise of land grants, came to the Bahamas from the southern American colonies in the wake of the English defeat in the Revolutionary War. This influx profoundly affected the islands. A number of prominent Bahamians today are the descendants of loyalists or their slaves. As a reward for his efforts, Deveaux was given acreage on both New Providence and Cat Island. Other loyalists set up cotton plantations on various islands, and slaves soon became the majority of the population.

Emancipation and Decline

In the 1780s well over 100 cotton plantations were founded and flourished around the Bahamas. Prosperity from the land finally seemed a possibility. But by the end of the century cotton had fallen victim to a devastating plague of chenille bugs and exhaustion of the weak soil. Most of the planters left the islands and depression returned, only partly relieved by "wrecking," the freelance business of salvaging cargo from the ships forever running aground in the dangerous Bahamian waters. (Some ships were deliberately misguided by lights on shore; Nassau harbor did not have a proper lighthouse until 1816).

Nassau became a free port in 1787, sparking a surge in trading activity. Loyalists built a number of the attractive colonial-style

A bust and plaque memorializes Sir Milo Butler in Parliament Square, Nassau.

homes and public buildings still standing today, and during the War of 1812, privateers enjoyed another profitable spell against American vessels.

Slavery in the Bahamas was not as widespread or as vicious as on many sugar islands in the Caribbean. Some slaves were voluntarily freed or sold their liberty by loyalist owners. After 1804, no slaves were imported into the Bahamas. By 1822, the first registration counted 10,808 slaves on the 17 inhabited islands or island clusters. After Parliament in London abolished slavery in 1833, there was a transitional apprenticeship period of 5 years before all slaves in the colony became fully free on 1 August 1838. This included a few thousand slaves from ships captured by the Royal Navy. They were housed in specially founded settlements on New Providence and the Out Islands.

Loading up: Marsh Harbour in Great Abaco is now a busy port.

Civil War Blockade Running

Over the centuries, trouble on the nearby American continent has often meant good news for the Bahamas. When Lincoln ordered a blockade of the southern states in 1861 after the outbreak of the Civil War, the Bahamas quickly boomed. Nassau harbor was busy with ships unloading Confederate cotton and tobacco and taking aboard arms, medicine, and manufactured goods, mainly from Europe, to be run back through the northern blockade. As the war went on, speedy and camouflaged contraband vessels were built to slip past the ever-increasing Federal patrols. Profits from blockade running were incredible, and Nassau went wild. But the extravagant parties and carefree spending stopped abruptly with the North's victory in 1865. Late the following year an immense hurricane sent a tidal wave over Hog Island (today Paradise Island), smashing Nassau's flimsy buildings and ruining crops. Other islands were also devastated. As the Bahamas sank back into economic doldrums, citizens turned to agriculture, fishing, or salt raking. The spread of lighthouses and decent navigational charts had crippled the old standby, the wrecking trade.

For a time a new fiber called sisal seemed promising. But Bahamian soil was too poor and Mexico grew a better plant. Neville Chamberlain, future British Prime Minister, took over his family's sisal operation on Andros in the 1890s. It failed, the natives said, because of that island's evil elves called *chickcharnies,* who cast a spell on the family for disturbing the land. Hopes were raised, and also fizzled, over Bahamian citrus and pineapple. Sponging, another vitally important industry at the end of the 19th century, also had setbacks. A hurricane in 1839 drowned some 300 sponge fishermen in the 'mud' off Andros, and a devastating fungus some 40 years later killed almost all the sponges.

The 20th Century

Desperate for work, perhaps 20 percent of the Bahamian population left to take construction jobs in Florida between the turn of the century and World War I. During that war hundreds of Bahamians saw active service with British forces. The islands suffered food shortages and a serious bank failure, but nothing more threatening militarily than rumors of German submarines offshore.

Prohibition brought gloom to millions of Americans, but for the Bahamas it brought the biggest bonanza in history. At the end of 1919, Congress passed the Volstead Act outlawing the manufacture, sale, or transport of intoxicating beverages. The Bahamian islands (where the temperance crusade never had much chance) were perfectly placed to help thirsty Americans. For 14 years, until the controversial law was finally repealed, bootlegging changed Nassau, West End on Grand Bahama, and Bimini beyond recognition. With just as much gusto as they'd shown in the past for wrecking, privateering, and blockade running, Bahamians took to the seas with illegal liquor. Trying to outwit the US Coast Guard was risky but enormously profitable. Fortunes were made by respected Bahamian families turned liquor merchants, rum-running boat captains, notorious criminals, shady ladies, and the Bahamas government (which collected duty on temporarily imported drink).

Liquor money bought Nassau better houses, churches, lighting, water, roads, sewers, docks, and hotels. The city's first gambling casino opened in 1920; the first daily air service from Miami began in 1929; the yacht set decided Nassau was fashionable, and many wealthy Americans as well as Prohibition millionaires built homes on the islands.

When the boom suddenly came to an end with the worldwide depression and the repeal of Prohibition in 1933, unemployment rose again, despite the first significant tourism the Bahamas had known.

In some respects, World War II put the Bahamas on the international map. The colony was chosen to have two of the sites Britain leased to the United States under Franklin D. Roosevelt's "destroyers for bases" deal in 1940. Allied forces operated submarine-hunting and air-sea rescue stations on the islands; Royal Air Force pilots and Royal Navy frogmen were trained here, and much trans-Atlantic air traffic passed through the Bahamas.

Then, to the astonishment of the local populace, the Duke of Windsor, having given up his throne for an American divorcée, was named governor of the little colony in 1940. He and the Duchess remained until 1945.

In 1943 the Duke intervened in the investigation of the murder of Canadian multimillionaire Sir Harry Oakes, a longtime benefactor

View from the past: an old stone window, Fort Charlotte, Nassau.

of the Bahamas who gave his name to Nassau's first airfield. The sensational case, never solved, made world headlines for the Bahamas and is still discussed today.

After the construction of the first wartime American air bases on New Providence was completed, thousands of Bahamians left to work on farms and in factories in the United States, a migration that continued well into the postwar era. But employment opportunities began to grow at home. From

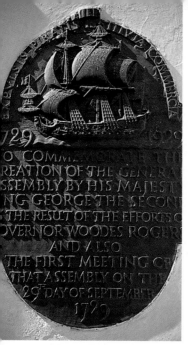

This plaque in Nassau's Parliament Square indicates the influence of King George II.

1950, a promotion campaign under Sir Stafford Sands was hugely successful in attracting tourists to the Bahamas. Denied the sun, sand, and sin of Cuba by Fidel Castro's takeover in 1959, hundreds of thousands of American vacationers set their sights on the Bahamas. The influx was spurred by gambling, airport and harbor improvement on the major islands, and the creation of the modern city of Freeport (which had been set in motion by the so-called Hawksbill Creek Agreement of 1955). Resort hotels began to appear and the advent of air-conditioning improved the often stifling humidity of summer.

Under a new constitution in 1964, the colony was given self-government with a ministerial-parliamentary system. In 1967 elections, the Progressive Liberal Party was victorious, its leader Lynden O. Pindling becoming premier. Following a constitutional conference in London, the Bahamas became fully independent on July 10, 1973, and is now a member of the United Nations and the British Commonwealth. In August 1992 the Progressive Liberal Party, still headed by Lynden O. Pindling, was toppled by the

Free National Movement after 25 years in power. Today's prime minister is Hubert Ingraham.

Since independence the Bahamas has kept British systems of judiciary and government yet has moved closer economically to its near neighbor, the US. The Bahamian Government has deliberately pursued tourism as the major industry of the Bahamian commonwealth and is happy to welcome many millions of visitors to its shores. The growth in cruise traffic has been particularly strong. The other islands, called the Family Islands by the government but generally referred to as the Out Islands by the tourist trade, have not shared this huge growth in numbers of visitors. Together they offer tourists almost any form of vacation experience, from the bustle of the busy city to the silence of the desert island.

In the 1990s the Bahamian Government began working on ways to expand the country's economic base. While tourism remains a top priority—the opening of the vast Atlantis resort on Paradise Island leaves little doubt about that—a number of measures have also been taken to make the country's laws and tax codes more attractive to offshore investors. As a result, money has been making its way into financial institutions on the Bahamas from around the world, and a large number of foreign banks have opened brand-new air-conditioned offices surrounded by carefully manicured gardens.

One of the major questions still facing the Bahamas is how to accommodate the increasing numbers of tourists while still preserving the special architectural and social heritage of the Out Islands, as well as of the major towns like Nassau. Will it be possible to enjoy the natural splendors of places like Inagua without upsetting the delicate balance of nature? At the moment, the thinking is that it's perhaps best to leave these smaller, less developed islands in peace.

Historical Landmarks

1492   Columbus sights San Salvador, the first land of the "New World."

1629   Charles I grants the Bahamas to Sir Robert Heath.

1648   The Eleutherian Adventurers found a colony on Eleuthera.

1666   William Sayle founds a settlement on New Providence, which later becomes Nassau.

Late 1600s Pirates rule the seas around the Bahamas.

1718   Ex-privateer Captain Woodes Rogers is named first Governor of the English Crown Colony of The Bahamas.

1782   The Spanish occupy the Bahamas.

1783   The Treaty of Versailles gives the Bahamas back to Britain. Loyalists from the newly independent United States emigrate to the Bahamas; most settle on the Abaco Cays.

1790s   Cotton plantations established across the islands and the first slaves are brought to work on them.

1787   Nassau becomes a free port.

1838   Slavery is abolished.

1861   The Bahamas benefits from the American Civil War by running the Union blockade to trade with the Confederates.

1919   The Volstead Act establishes Prohibition in the US; the Bahamas begins smuggling into the US and attracts thirsty American tourists.

1940   Areas of the Bahamas are leased to the US military for use as bases.

1955   The Hawksbill Creek Agreement advances the development of Grand Bahama and leads to the development of the planned city of Freeport.

1973   Bahamas becomes an independent nation.

WHERE TO GO

NEW PROVIDENCE

It's not the largest of the Bahamas islands and not the most stunningly beautiful, yet when most people think of the Bahamas they first think of New Providence or its major town, **Nassau**. The island is only 80 square miles in size yet 180,000 of the 280,000 Bahamians lives here. The town and its port and international airport are the hub for every activity in the Bahamas. Government, administration, taxes, and furniture shipments for new homes all start from here and radiate out to the other islands. New Providence also attracts over 3 million visitors every year, and Nassau is one of the main cruise ports of the Caribbean. The island is a magnet for fun seekers and serious shoppers, and it serves both very well.

> One thing which one notices about the Bahamian people is their ready smiles.

Nassau

Nassau town has a fine pedigree dating back through colonial times, and the compact town center still has the feel of life under the English. Out in the natural harbor, which offered shelter to many a pirate ship, is a major port that can accommodate 15 large cruise ships at one time. This capacity was created in 1965 when public money was invested to dredge the port, specifically to allow bigger ships to enter. The huge vessels, hundreds of feet high, dwarf the towns buildings, which regulations set at a maximum of three stories, and create one of the most effective juxtapositions of modernity and history found anywhere in the world. The cruise port at **Prince George Wharf** brings in by far the majority of visitors to the Bahamas.

There's plenty to buy in Nassau, one of the major cruise ports of the Caribbean, and a hot spot for shopping.

Immediately in front of the cruise port you'll find a line of **horse-drawn surreys** waiting to offer you a genteel tour along the historic streets. The horses wait under the cooling shade for their next customers. (In the hot summer months the horses are not allowed to work from 2–4pm.) The horses trot slowly past all the sights in town, but you can also easily stroll around yourself and see everything in a couple of hours—if you're not seduced by the many shopping opportunities between the docks and the historic old town.

The first sight that will attract your attention is the **Straw Market** on Market Plaza, which backs onto Woodes Rodgers Walk. For many years this has been the showcase for Bahamian handicrafts. Straw goods, including baskets and mats, are favorite souvenirs; each island produces straw goods in its own style and patterns. Bestsellers are hats, dolls, bags, and

Highlights of New Providence

Ardastra Gardens. *Chippingham Road, Nassau; Tel. 323-5806*. Open daily 9am–5pm. The flamingo show takes place daily at 11am, 2pm, and 4pm. Admission: adults $10, children $5.

Balcony House. *Market Street, Nassau; Tel. 326-2566*. Open Mon, Wed, Fri 10am–1pm, 2–4pm.

Blue Lagoon Dolphin Experience. *Nassau; Tel. 363-1003*. Open daily 8am–5:30pm. Basic program: $29.

Changing of the Guard. *Outside Government House, Blue Hill Road*. Every two weeks, the Police Band performs at 10am.

The Cloisters. *Paradise Island, Nassau*. Open at all times unless booked for a private function. Admission free.

Crystal Cay Marine Park. *Silver Cay; Tel. 328-1036*. Open daily Apr–Oct 9am–6pm, Nov–Mar 9am–5:30pm. Admission: adults $16, children $11.

The Dig at Atlantis Resort. *Paradise Island, Nassau; Tel. 363-3000*. A day pass is required for non-guests, $25 per person.

Fort Charlotte. *Off West Bay Street, Nassau; Tel. 322-7500*. Open Mon–Sat 8:30am–4pm. Admission free.

Nassau Public Library and Museum. *Shirley Street; Tel. 322-4907*. Open Mon–Thur 10am–8pm, Fri 10am–5pm, Sat 10am–4pm.

Pirates of Nassau. *Corner of King Street and George Street, Nassau; Tel. 356-3759*. Open Mon–Sat 9am–5pm. Admission: $12 for adults, two children go free with each adult.

The Pompey Museum. *Vendue House, Bay Street, Nassau; Tel. 326-2566*. Open Mon–Fri 10am–4:30pm, Sat 10am–1pm; closed for lunch Mon, Wed, Fri 1–2pm. Admission: adults $1, children 50¢.

The Water Tower. *Beside Fort Fincastle, Elizabeth Avenue, Nassau; Tel. 322-2442*. Call for hours of operation. Admission 50¢.

Echoes of the past; this marble statue of Queen Victoria graces Parliament Square.

baskets. There is some exquisite work to be found, but be aware that with a decline in basket-making throughout the Bahamas, an increasing number of articles are imported from the Far East; most of these are at the cheaper end of the scale. The ubiquitous modern souvenir, the T-shirt, is also available, with an almost limitless number of pictures, patterns, and slogans. The ladies who run the stalls are easy-going and seem to have limitless enthusiasm for the next sale. You'll hear numerous calls of "Hey, honey, come look for something nice here."

The straw market fronts onto **Bay Street**, one of the leading duty-free shopping capitals of the world. Only a few years ago this street was the domain of the Bay Street Boys, a small group of men who controlled all economic activity in the Bahamas; now Bay Street seduces visitors with huge sparkling gems, hundreds of ounces of gold, and the smell of a thousand designer fragrances. The façades of the pretty 18th-century shops hide modern air-conditioned shopping palaces piled high with luxury goods.

Many visitors, especially those with only a few hours to spare, go no farther than the shops of Nassau—shopping for a bargain can be exhausting. It would be a shame, however, not to explore what the rest of Nassau has to offer, as there are a number of historic gems to be discovered in and around the town. The Bahamian people appreciate and enjoy the many touches of colonial history retained from its days as part of the British Empire. **Rawson Square**, just in front of the entrance to Prince George Wharf, is a good place to start your tour. The tourist information office here can arm you with leaflets and maps that will help you make the most of your day. Directly opposite Rawson Square, across Bay Street, are the **Public Buildings of Parliament Square**, which have been in continuous use since 1812. They were modeled on the governmental complex in New Bern, capital of the North Carolina colony two centuries ago. A marble statue of a young, seated Queen Victoria in front recalls the era of British rule. The two chambers of the modern House of Assembly meet in the so-called western building (on the right side if you're facing from the square); the public-records office and government publications department are housed in the other historic buildings. Behind them in modern edifices are the Law Courts. Here you may find yourself in the middle of a parade to open parliament or convene the courts. The smart uniforms and pomp are taken directly from British ceremonial activities, but the ambiance is truly Bahamian. Check with the Tourist Board for dates of ceremonial occasions, all of which happen frequently.

> **Complain about the traffic in Nassau; everybody else does. Although by London or New York standards the town has only minor problems, the situation has steadily worsened in recent years and it is a constant source of conversation among Bahamians on almost every island.**

Behind the modern law court complex is the **Nassau Public Library**, interesting because it used to be the island's jail. The octagonal structure on Shirley Street dates from 1797 and has a pretty exterior, but the interior is more fascinating.

The old cells were retained when the structure became the library in 1873 and books line every wall, replacing prisoners and creating private reading areas. The library museum also has a collection of old maps and charts used to navigate the waters around the Bahamas.

If you're walking, continue east along Shirley Street until you reach Elizabeth Avenue, and turn right. The land rises suddenly here. This area, behind the downtown area, had been used to great strategic effect by the British. **Fort Fincastle** was built atop the rise in 1793 to watch the shipping lanes and protect Nassau harbor. The tiny fort is shaped like the prow of a ship, though there is hardly enough room to fit a football team, never mind a unit of the queen's soldiery. To reach the fort you must climb the **Queen's Staircase**, an artificial narrow gorge leading to 65 steps that climb a hillside. Both the gorge and the staircase, created to allow soldiers to reach or leave the fort quickly, were hewn from the solid limestone by a contingent of slave workers. At the top of the staircase and next to the fort, the **Water Tower** offers a bird's-eye view over Nassau, Paradise Island, and most of the rest of New Providence. A small elevator in the concrete structure will carry you 125 ft (38 m) to the top. Don't forget your camera.

> Tune your body clock to Bahamian time, not an actual hour on the clock but a state of mind— slow and relaxed, though not so slow that nothing gets done.

After a visit to the tower, return to the compact town center. Stroll along any street and you'll bump into fine historic buildings; several date from the late 1700s and most are painted in pretty pastels that cheerfully reflect the bright Bahamian sunlight. Pink-and-white **Balcony House** on Market Street is a particularly fine example. The oldest wooden house on the island—it was built by shipwrights around 1790 of American soft cedar—it has been restored and is now a museum that offers a delightful view of life in well-to-do Nassau in the 18th century. Once a private home visited by the likes of the Duke of Windsor and Winston Churchill, **Graycliff Mansion** on West Hill Street is now a fine hotel with a well regarded menu and wine list. Many of the original Georgian Colonial features have been retained, and a collection of photographs provide guests and visitors with a glimpse into the building's genteel past.

Vendue House, at the western end of Bay Street, at the corner of George Street, was once the site of the Nassau slave auction. It now houses the **Pompey Museum of Slavery and Emancipation**. The pale pink stone house is unassuming, but the interior tells of the plight of slaves on the islands and of the positive work that was undertaken in the years following emancipation.

Fort Fincastle, shaped like the prow of a ship, stands watch over Nassau harbor.

It's not all tall tales and costumes…Nassau's pirate history is all too real, and may inspire you to do a little digging!

The **Pirates of Nassau** attraction at the corner of George and Marlborough Streets brings to life the dramatic and exciting world of the pirates. The building itself dates from the 18th century; the attraction inside recreates the Nassau quayside of the 17th century. A three-quarter-size French corvette ship and quayside buildings have been stunningly brought to life. As you walk along the "dock," costumed staff act out the roles of shipmate and pirate and regale you with tales of their everyday lives and deeds. Visitors then step inside the 75-ft- (23-m-) long vessel to examine the paraphernalia of the pirate's trade that line the corridors and decks. Treasure chests mix with rum casks, and pirates tell of their lives at sea in the lonely and dangerous times. Listen to the groaning of injured pirates and witness the rudimentary and unsanitary surgical techniques that led to so many deaths—the ship's carpenter doubled as surgeon. Read about the crew's diet of "salmagun-di," a stew of pickled herrings, meat, and eggs mixed with wine and vinegar, which served to both preserve the protein and disguise the taste. Battle scenes are vividly recreated, and visitors find out the truth about what finally became of some of the most famous pirates.

The next street to the west is Blue Hill Road. About 1,640 ft (500 m) south of Shirley Street, opposite Graycliff Mansion, stands **Government House**, the official residence of the Governor-General, painted in the same shade of pink as the buildings of Parliament Square. At the north gate is a statue of Christopher Columbus in a rather dashing pose reminiscent of Errol Flynn in one of his swashbuckling films. Once every two weeks there is a solemn **Changing of the Guard** parade, similar to the one at Buckingham Palace in London, performed to the accompaniment of the Police Band. On the last Friday of the month from January to June all visitors to the island are invited to attend a huge tea party on the grounds.

Paradise Island

Across Nassau Harbour north of the town is **Paradise Island**, known until the 1940s as Hog Island. For many centuries the

---

Buried Treasure

Nassau was one of the most popular towns in the Caribbean with the pirates who terrorized the seas. Dubloons and "pieces of eight," as well as gold and jewels worth millions of dollars at today's prices, were plundered and wagered in illicit gambling sessions, and then used to fund new expeditions. A great deal of treasure is still not accounted for, however, and where better to hide it than on the remote and uninhabited cays of the Bahamas. Who knows? There may be a fortune hidden just below your beach towel!

Pristine beaches and turquoise water—they don't call it Paradise Island for nothing!

island simply acted as a protective barrier against bad weather and attack from invaders. Its recent history is fascinating: In the 1930s it was owned by Swedish millionaire Axel Wenner-Gren, an arms manufacturer who was found to be a Nazi sympathizer. He sold the island to Huntingdon Hartford, who changed the name from Hog to Paradise and created a beautiful private retreat, now the Ocean Club Hotel. Later gangster Per Lansky began the process that transformed the island from a private sanctuary with magnificent homes into a playground for tourists. The wonderful beaches, such as Cabbage Beach on the northern coast, were the focus of the development. The first hotels began to appear in the 1960s when gambling was a lure to the rich and famous. As Paradise Island saw owners Donald Trump and Merv Griffin come and go, it went through a continuing series of developments and re-developments.

Today Paradise Island may be close to fulfilling the dream of the perfect vacation playground. It has many of the essential ingredients needed: fine white-sand beaches, a protected marina, a golf course, a group of fine hotels, and perhaps the biggest adult playground this side of Las Vegas. The brainchild of the Sol Group, **Atlantis Paradise Island** is a new concept in resorts—it's a huge hotel with an amazing theme park and entertainment village all on one site. The resort takes its name, and inspiration, from the lost city of Atlantis, said by some to lie off the coast of Bimini. This theme runs throughout the whole resort. The vast open foyers and public areas of the hotel have high columns of cathedral-like dimensions; the walkways and outside terraces recall Mayan

---

The Lost World of Atlantis

The legend of Atlantis is well known—the richest and most cultured city in the world during its heyday, it suffered a great catastrophe and sank into the sea, its whereabouts lost in the mists of time.

Archaeologists and explorers have been searching for clues to its location or even solid evidence that it existed at all. Several locations have been proposed, the most impressive put the location at Santorini, the small Greek island that was destroyed by a powerful earthquake. In 1969, however, two explorers diving in the waters off Bimini discovered a strange chain of flat interlocking stone slabs that looked remarkably like an ancient road. Excitement grew in the Bahamas that Atlantis was really in their waters, but the deep has still to give up many more secrets if the truth is ever to be known. Until then, the dream of what Atlantis may have looked like and how her people lived is brought to life at Atlantis Paradise Island, the theme park (see above) and aquarium, where you can indulge your fantasies.

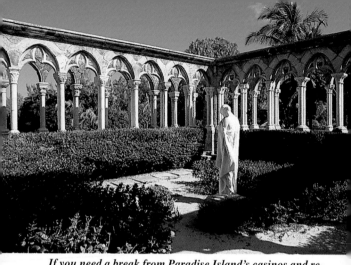

If you need a break from Paradise Island's casinos and resorts, peaceful contemplation awaits you in The Cloisters.

temples, with large stones covering the façade. Waterfalls literally or figuratively cascade to give a feeling of a city just having risen from the ocean. Man-made sheltered lagoons provide for safe swimming, snorkeling, and sunbathing.

The masterpiece of the whole Atlantis complex is the enormous **Aquarium**, which can be viewed from almost any point in the resort—from the rooms above in the towers, from ground level, and from below ground. Within the Aquarium is an area called the **Dig**, a spectacular underwater environment complete with sunken "treasures," vast stone columns, fallen temples, and godlike figures, all intended to show what Atlantis might look like while being excavated. The entire attraction has then been filled with sea water and a complete ecosystem of fish and crustaceans, 100,000 in all.

Sharks and rays patrol the waterways, eels and lobsters lurk in the crevices and fissures. A truly awe-inspiring sight.

The resort boasts 20 restaurants, three shopping malls, and a vast casino area. Outside, water slides, nature trails, and swimming pools indicate that no expense has been spared to create the ultimate playground for all age groups. Many visitors to the Bahamas drop in just to marvel at the artistry and technical skill that was employed to create this complex. Non-guests must pay a fee to enjoy the resort facilities and an extra fee for a visit to the Dig.

At the eastern end of Paradise Island stands a much older structure that offers the opportunity for restful contemplation. **The Cloisters** are the remains of a 14th-century monastery that was bought in France by Huntingdon Hartford, taken apart, and rebuilt in the grounds of his home, now the Ocean Club hotel. Hartford set the small courtyard on a rise several hundred yards away from the house and created an elaborate garden to lead to the edifice. The Versailles Gardens, based on Louis XIV's formal palace gardens outside Paris, have terraces, fountains, and statues that provide a soothing vista, leading the eye from the house to the cloisters. It is possible to visit the Cloisters during daylight hours—they stand next to the only road that traverses the island—but they are used regularly for wedding ceremonies, so you might find them closed.

Paradise Island is connected to New Providence by two bridges that rise high into the air to allow boat traffic to pass beneath. One bridge carries traffic on to the island, the other takes traffic back to Nassau (there is a small toll for vehicles). At the foot of the bridges is a small quay where you can catch a ferry to Woodes Rogers Walk in Nassau port. This is also the docking point for boats to **Blue Lagoon and the Dolphin Experience**. A small cay just a 20-minute boat ride from Paradise Island, Blue Lagoon is the site of a facility where you can swim with the dolphins or help the staff look after the animals for a day. Boats leave several times a day.

No public buses—jitneys—are allowed over the toll bridge to Paradise Island. You'll need to take a taxi to and from Nassau if you don't use the ferry. Once on the island, however, you can use the public bus service, which runs the length of the island, linking the hotels with the quayside and the small shopping center.

Underneath the bridges in the harbor is a small island called **Potter's Cay**. This is where fishing boats and mail boats dock and where real Bahamian life happens. Stalls sell fresh conch salad and people sit and wait for the night's sailing. The harbor master's office here can help you with mailboat schedules and prices.

In the pink: these endangered pink flamingos have found themselves a happy home in the Ardastra Zoo.

Beyond Nassau

There are a number of interesting attractions outside of Nassau that make it worthwhile to rent a car or hire a taxi for the day.

West of Nassau

Head west out of Nassau and within a couple of minutes you'll encounter three very different attractions. There's no missing the austere gray ramparts of **Fort Charlotte**, which guards the western approaches to Nassau Harbour. Built by Lord Dunmore in 1787–89, during the Napoleonic Wars, and named after the wife of George III, this is the largest fort in the Bahamas. But not one shot was ever fired from here in anger—the only volleys ever launched were part of ceremonial salutes. Life must have been pretty boring for the soldiers as many had the time to carve their names in the stones along the battlements. Guides escort visitors around the interior of the fort as well as through the dungeons, which, thankfully, saw little torture. In fact Fort Charlotte is well regarded by New Providence residents as a shelter during hurricanes.

Nearby is **Ardastra Gardens, Zoo, and Conservation Centre**, a landscaped park famed for its pink flamingos, which are paraded three times a day into a small enclosure to offer visitors a closer look. These birds, once common in certain Bahamian islands, are now disappearing, though the reasons for the decline are disputed. Another endangered species, the Bahamian Parrot, is under threat from loss of habitat. The Gardens is one of only a small number of centers that has developed a breeding program for this vocal and gregarious bird in the hope of replenishing colonies in the wild. There are many more species of Caribbean mammals, reptiles, birds, and fish to find as you explore the 5½ acres of tropical parkland.

Go under without getting wet at the underwater observatory in Crystal Cay.

Head back to the main coast road and you will find two small cays lying immediately offshore. The first is **Arawak Cay**, home to the local fishing fleet. A number of colorful shacks line the approach road where you can buy conch and fried fish, always fresh and always delicious. Weekends can be busy with local families. Travel through Arawak Cay to reach Silver Cay, where there is a small resort with a pretty beach. Here you will find **Crystal Cay**, site of a marine park where you can take a close look at the undersea world without getting wet. A man-made coral reef has been created on the sea bottom and you can watch all the marine activity from an underwater observatory. The reef attracts many kinds of aquatic creatures that are free to come and go as they please. The observatory looks decidedly futuristic and can be seen quite clearly from the road as you travel along the coast. Other activities at Crystal Cay include a sea turtle environment, a touch pool where you can stroke a sting ray or pet a conch, and a snorkel trail, if you want to get into the water yourself.

A little further west along the coast you will find **Cable Beach**, the third main center of tourism on New Providence. Several luxury hotels line the shore, only 5 minutes by car from central Nassau. The Nassau Marriott Resort Hotel attracts many visitors with its casino, stage shows, and restaurants. The

Cable Beach "strip" is under continual development, and a number of private restaurants have opened recently to provide alternatives for guests staying at the resorts.

East of Nassau

The territory east and southeast of Nassau has seen a great deal of development in the last twenty years; many of the major residential areas that have sprung up hold little interest for visitors. One legacy of the past is **Blackbeard's Tower**, said to have been a lookout post for the famous pirate. It is a little careworn and forlorn today and may be worth visiting only for its view of the harbor. Guarding the eastern entrance to Nassau harbor is tiny **Fort Montague**, least visited of the old colonial fortifications. It now looks out towards the pleasure palaces of Paradise Island.

GRAND BAHAMA

Northwest of New Providence, **Grand Bahama Island** was largely ignored through colonial history and was for a long time a comparative backwater. That it is now the second most popular tourist destination in the Bahamas is all due to the forethought of one man—and a great deal of investment made since 1955. The British had little interest in developing Grand Bahama, but the island lies only 55 miles from the Florida coast, and in the post–World War II period it finally attracted the attention of developers. As the economy of the US grew and Bahamian–US trade increased, a group of businessmen, led by Wallace Groves, saw the potential in the development of Grand Bahama.

In 1955 the British government signed the Hawksbill Agreement, which gave Groves 50,000 acres (20,000 hectares) of land and a concession to import duty-free goods. In return Groves agreed to build a deep-water harbor and to encourage business development. First there was boom, then there was bust, but a container port opened in the 1990s is breathing new life into the flagging commercial sector. The opening of the first casino in 1964 sparked the tourist boom and, since then, Grand Bahama has been busy developing as a tourist "mecca." Its modernity and the close links with the US create a totally different atmosphere and style compared to what you'll find in New Providence, and many visitors enjoy the more "American" feel.

Freeport-Lucaya

The main settlement on Grand Bahama, **Freeport-Lucaya** is in fact two separate towns that have now grown together. In theory Freeport was the commercial center and Lucaya the coastal resort. In reality the two towns now mix so success-

---

Highlights of Grand Bahama

Garden of the Groves. *Corner of Midshipman Road and Magellan Drive; Tel. 352-4045.* Open Mon–Fri 9am–4pm, Sat, Sun, and holidays 10am–4pm. Admission: adults $5, children $2.50.

Lucaya National Park. *Midshipman Road, 8 miles east of Freeport/Lucaya.* Open during daylight hours. Admission free.

The Perfume Factory. *Freeport; Tel. 352-9391.* Free five-minute guided tours Mon– Fri 10am–5:30pm.

Rand Nature Centre and Memorial Gardens. *East Settlers Way, Freeport; Tel. 352—5438.* Open Mon–Fri 9am–4pm, Sat 9am–1pm. Guided tours Mon–Fri at 10am and 2pm.

UNEXSO Dolphin Experience. *Next to Port Lucaya; Tel. 373-1250, in the US 800-992-DIVE or (305) 351-9889.* Museum open daily 9–5. Basic program: $29; diving with dolphins: $105.

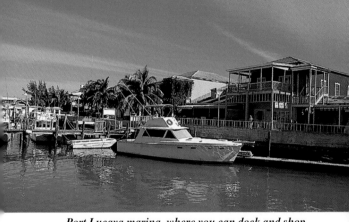

Port Lucaya marina, where you can dock and shop (duty-free) 'til you drop!

fully it is difficult to tell where the dividing line is. Most of the island's 40,000 people live here and the towns continue to develop. There are no historical attractions here but Freeport-Lucaya is happy to offer the alternative of unashamed hedonistic pleasure and relaxation.

Not surprisingly for a duty-free island, shopping plays a large part in a trip to Grand Bahama. **International Bazaar** in Freeport takes you on a shopping trip around the world. Enter the bazaar through the red Japanese Torii or "welcome gate" and you can visit France, Africa, and India, all within a few minutes. Unusual offerings such as rare stamps can be found among the standard duty-free shops that carry the most exclusive names in watches, jewelry, and perfume. Behind the South American area you'll find the **Perfume Factory**, where you can create your own personal fragrance. Mix essential oils to balance with your skin and give a name to your exclusive product. You can even record the recipe on computer so that you can

Spin and win! You might get lucky at the Princess Casino in Grand Bahama.

re-order the exact fragrance at a later date. The "factory" is set in a pretty 18th-century colonial mansion replica; five-minute tours take visitors into the small commercial production plant, where some of the Factory's own signature perfumes are made.

Make your way past the Continental Pavilion at the back of the International Bazaar to reach **Goombay Market**. Here you'll find an amazing range of straw work, wooden carvings, and other handicrafts. There are over 100 stalls, so it's a great place to barter for a bargain.

Next door to the International Bazaar is the **Princess Casino** with its distinctive Moorish domes. You'll be able to play alongside the "high rollers" at the roulette or craps tables or put a few coins in the slot machines. There is also a theater that hosts nightly dance show performances. The casino is part of the complex of the Bahamas Princess Resort and Casino, where you'll also find a country club and two excellent 18-hole golf courses.

Lucaya is set on a fine sandy beach and the expansive **Port Lucaya** marina gives the whole resort a very nautical feel. A number of large hotels line the Lucayan Beach, their massive façades softened by the hundreds of masts of the yachts moored on the inlet. As of late 1999, the casinos and many of the hotels were being given a facelift and three of the larger hotels on the waterfront were being reconfigured into a single complex.

Port Lucaya Marketplace is the center of all activity for the town. During the day the duty-free shops in this Mediterranean-style shopping village tempt shoppers with jewelry, clothing, and perfume; colorful wooden huts house craft stalls selling straw work and carvings. As the sun sinks people gather at the marketplace after a day on the beach or sailing offshore. The streets come alive as bars and restaurants fill up and bands play live music at the Count Basie Bandstand in a square adjoining the marina.

On the south side of the marina, accessible from the main beach road, is the **Underwater Explorers Society** or **UNEXSO**. The oldest diving organization in the Bahamas, UNEXSO provides diving experience sessions and training courses. The large square building contains a diving pool and decompression chamber; those with no interest in actually practicing the sport can visit the museum, which charts the development of diving to the modern SCUBA (**s**elf-**c**ontained **u**nderwater **b**reathing **a**pparatus) method developed by Jacques Cousteau in the 1930s. There is also a good restaurant on site, the Brass Helmet. A short boatride from Port Lucaya takes you to **Sanctuary Bay** and the **UNEXSO Dolphin Experience**. A family

People to People

The Bahamas Tourist Board has established a "meet-the-people" program that provides visitors with a chance to discover how ordinary Bahamians live. Participating families open their homes to visitors, and if you have a special interest, the Ministry of Tourism will match you with individuals or families that share your passion. This is a wonderful way to experience the everyday lives of your hosts. For more information, call 326-5371.

Lucaya's imaginatively landscaped Garden of the Groves is a delight.

of bottlenose dolphins have set up home here. You can linger by the side of the bay and hope they come to you, get in the water and swim with them, or spend a day as an assistant trainer and help the staff care for these gentle creatures.

Just north of the Marina is the **Lucayan Golf and Country Club**, which has some of the best-groomed greens in the Bahamas and a very good restaurant for those who want to watch rather than play—diners enjoy panoramic views over the driving range and several holes.

Freeport-Lucaya may be a modern town of concrete and tarmac, but within the city limits are two natural areas that could be a million miles away from the bustle of the shops and large hotels. **Rand Memorial Nature Centre**, on 100 acres of land on East Settlers Way to the east of Freeport, is used as a resource for students on the island, but there's nothing dry and academic about it. Here you can learn about the plants native to the Bahamas and find out which ones were used for bush medicine and for what purpose. A flock of flamingos and numerous other native bird species make their home here.

To the east of Lucaya on Midshipman Road is **Parrot Jungle's Garden of the Groves**. This beautiful garden was created in tribute to Wallace Groves and his wife, and the 11 acres (4½ hectares) contain more than 10,000 different plant species. The landscaping is delightful, with ponds, waterfalls, and shady places to sit and enjoy the view. A pretty chapel atop a small hill offers a fine vantage point over the whole park. For the child in all of us the small petting zoo is great fun.

Beyond Freeport-Lucaya

Grand Bahama is relatively easy to explore by car, with only one major road running east to McLean's Town and another north to West End.

Eastern Grand Bahama

As you head east out of town you'll soon leave the trappings of modernity behind and find yourself on a good road through acres of Bahamian forest. The road crosses a number of canals, and just off the south coast is **Petersons Cay**, a tiny but beautiful coral cay with a beach—a great spot for a day of swimming, snorkeling, sunbathing, and picnicking.

After traveling approximately 10 miles on the main road you'll come to **Lucaya National Park** (there's a small parking lot on your left). The 40-acre (16-hectare) park sits on both sides of the main road and protects a range of Bahamian ecosystems. Inland, trails lead to one of the largest surveyed cave systems in the world, much of which lies underwater. **Ben's Cave**, also known as Bats Cave for reasons that will be obvious when you enter, is the most accessible and in fact rather small. It links to the larger caves through subterranean tunnels. The pool in the bottom has layers of fresh water lying on top of salt water. Remains of several Lucayan Indians that were found at the cave entrance are now being studied in Nassau. The caves are also home to a rare species of crustacean, *spelonectes Lucayensis,* which is said to resemble a swim-

Endless summer: Gold Rock Beach continues for five heavenly miles, and changes dramatically from low to high tide.

ming centipede. Ben's Cave is closed during June and July to protect the bats during the breeding season.

From the right-hand side of the road, well-marked trails lead through the vegetation and out toward the coast, just a few hundred meters away (a line of casuarina trees marks the spot). Wooden walkways lead you farther out over a tidal mangrove swamp to **Gold Rock Beach**. One of the most beautiful beaches on the island, Gold Rock must really be seen at low tide to appreciate its full glory. At high tide a shallow layer of water, only a couple of inches deep, covers much of the beach, leaving only a narrow arc of sand above the waterline. This whole area can also be explored by bicycle or kayak or by taking an eco-tour. One of the companies that offers both eco- and cultural tours of the area is East End Adventures (Tel. 373-6662; e-mail <safari@batalnet.bs>).

Western Grand Bahama

Heading west from Freeport-Lucaya, you'll first travel past the cruise port and container port. Across from the entrance to the cruise port is Pier One Restaurant, where you can enjoy wonderful food and feed the sharks that gather underneath the terraces in the evening. Farther west, at Deadman's Reef, are the remains of an ancient Lucayan settlement discovered in 1996.

The Best Beaches

The Bahamas has literally thousands of wonderful secluded, sandy beaches, but many of these can only be reached by boat. The following is a list of the best, which are accessible to "land lubbers" as well as "yachties."

New Providence: *Cabbage Beach.* Right in the thick of the action, just steps away from the Atlantis Resort.

Grand Bahama: *Xanadu Beach.* A wide, gently sloping beach, sheltered from the waves, which makes it ideal for children. A comprehensive range of water sports activities are available for older kids and adults, and a small marketplace nearby has spots to shop for refreshments and souvenirs. The Xanadu Hotel is just a few hundred yards from the beach.

Gold Rock Beach. Five miles of white sand rippled by the regular tidal waters. Go when the tide is low to get the full effect of the beach's expanse.

The Abacos: *Treasure Cay Beach, Great Abaco Island.* Four miles of fine sand in a long crescent bay.

The Exumas: *Stocking Island.* A short ferry ride from George Town with sandy bays and coves for snorkeling.

Eleuthera: *Harbour Island.* Three miles of pink sand on the Atlantic coast.

Off the Beaten Track: *Fernandez Bay, on Cat Island; Great Guana Cay in the Abacos; The Exuma Land and Sea Park; Petersons Cay, off the coast of Grand Bahama*

The last settlement on the journey is **West End**, the oldest town on the island and today home to conch fishermen. Native Bahamians like to gather here on the weekends; there's always a "fish fry" (kind of like a large communal barbecue) and plenty of Kalik beer for sale. During the rest of the week, the village takes on a sleepy air. There's little evidence left of the bad old days of Prohibition when merchants and rum-runners here made fortunes smuggling liquor into the United States.

THE OUT ISLANDS

The Bahamas has traditionally been divided into three entities: New Providence, Grand Bahama, and all the rest of the islands, brought together under the collective name of the **Out Islands**, sometimes also referred to as the **Family Islands**. Most of the Out Islands are sparsely populated, and the traditional ways of island life are much more prevalent than they are on the two main islands. The rhythm of life is slower, communities are smaller, and time seems to stand still. What activity there is centers around the boats that continually move quietly in and out of the harbors.

Trips on the Mail Boat

A network of mail boats run from Nassau to the Out Islands, carrying everything from fruit to refrigerators to mattresses. For many local Bahamians it is the only way to get goods that are not available on their own island. The boats run a tight schedule and offer passenger service on a set timetable. Using this service provides a great way to see some of the more remote islands and to meet Bahamians. The only down side is that you need time—many services operate only once or twice a week and only service one island, so there's no chance of island hopping.

Conch of the day: Young boys plying their trade off the island of Grand Bahama.

The Abacos

A vaguely boomerang-shaped cluster of islands east of Grand Bahama, the Abacos offer perfect waters to explore by boat. Stretching for some 130 miles, the Abaco group consists of "mainland" **Little Abaco** and **Great Abaco** and an attendant string of hundreds of cays and islets. They are a sailor's paradise because the numerous safe anchorages and bays have been enhanced in modern times by comprehensive back-up facilities for sailors.

The Abacos were settled by English Loyalists during and after the American Revolution, who brought with them the distinctive architectural and decorative style of New England. These new immigrants made a living from cotton production and collecting sponges, but after several disastrous harvests and a fierce hurricane, a group of Abaconians left to create a sister community on Key West off the southern tip of Florida. The people of the Abacos remained staunchly pro-

British even into modern times, and of all the Bahamians they were the ones who expressed the most apprehension about the bid for independence in 1973.

Marsh Harbour, in the center of Great Abaco Island, is the proverbial heart of the Abacos. The town has a large harbor and has grown into a major sailing center. It is now the third-largest settlement in the Bahamas after Nassau and Freeport-Lucaya. Ships chandlers and hardware stores provide everything needed for the boats, and liquor stores and supermarkets have everything for the passengers and crew. A number of restaurants in and around the wide marina and bay provide opportunities for intimate dining experiences or rowdier live-music sing-alongs.

Although it is difficult to get to all the outlying cays without a boat (see page 98 for information about rentals), Marsh Har-

Candy-striped landmark—few photographers can resist the festive-looking lighthouse at Hope Town.

bour makes a good base for trips to the central section of the Abacos cays. A network of reliable ferry services runs to all the major cays, most of them no more than 30 minutes offshore.

Elbow Cay, southeast of Marsh Harbour, is the most popular, and its capital, **Hope Town**, is one of the most charming spots in the Bahamas. Yachts at anchor clutter the nearly circular harbor beneath a candy-striped lighthouse few photographers can resist. Rising 120 ft (37 m) above sea level, the **Hope Town Lighthouse** can be seen from a distance of 17 miles (27 km). When it was built in 1864 it helped drastically reduce the number of shipping accidents and shipwrecks, but it was unpopular with the native people who relied on lucrative salvage activities to make a living. It is one of only three manual lighthouses in the Bahamas and has to be turned throughout the day and night by a team of dedicated lighthouse workers. Climb the 101 steps to the top for fantastic views over the whole of Elbow Cay.

A pretty little village of pastel-colored clapboard houses, Hope Town is full of friendly locals. Kids run safely in the streets of the traffic-free town center and along the Queens Highway, only slightly wider than a sidewalk. Shoes are optional in the bars at the water's edge, and as the sun sets you'll hear a thousand stories here about the one that got away. Watch out for the sign "Tourists treated just like locals," for you'll soon feel as though you've lived here forever. You'll be exchanging greetings, and before you know it, life stories. The **Wyannie Malone Historical Museum** on Queens Highway is the place to find out more about these fascinating people and their home island.

To the northwest of Marsh Harbour is **Man-O-War Cay**, a small island of only 300 inhabitants famous for its boatyards. The dinghies and runabouts built here are hand-crafted; cotton is used to seal gaps between the wooden planks.

The boats are then sunk so that the wet cotton expands to make them watertight. Man-O-War is unusual in that it has always been a dry cay—no alcohol is sold anywhere.

Great Guana Cay, northwest of Man-O-War, has wonderful long, lonely beaches that run for miles along the island's eastern rim. A total of only 600 people live in the island's few small settlements, and the chief activity seems to be sitting under the large fig tree on the harbor front and gossiping. Sailors touring through the Bahamas love to anchor offshore here—this serene spot is one of the best places to switch off the rest of the world. Those who don't have their own transport can take one of the four ferries that run over every day from Marsh Harbour.

North of Marsh Harbour you'll see signs for **Treasure Cay**, which is, strictly speaking, a peninsula rather than a cay. The land here has been developed into one of the largest resort areas outside the two main islands. A large marina and 18-hole golf course attract a mixed group of people but the initial lure, and reason for the whole development, is **Treasure Beach**, one of the best in the whole Caribbean. This 6-mile arc of soft sand was for many years a Bahamian secret.

An airport north of Treasure Cay serves the resort and the northern offshore cays. A regular ferry service links with the flight times. Twenty minutes offshore is **Green Turtle Cay**. Much more lush than many of the other islands in the Bahamas, this hilly, 3-mile- (5-km-) long cay is covered with pine woodland that camouflages many of its houses and resorts. A Loyalist settlement dating from 1783—groups of colonists were evacuated from Savannah and Charleston along with black slaves who escaped their owners—Green Turtle in recent years has become a getaway for the rich and famous. The hotels here have all the luxuries you could ever need, yet you might feel as if you're a million miles away

Palm-fringed perfection awaits the beach lover in Elbow Cay, where doing next to nothing is "de rigueur."

from the worries of the world. The cay is small enough to explore on foot but most people choose to rent a golf cart or bicycle (your hotel can make the arrangements).

New Plymouth is the largest town on the cay. It really has only one main route, Parliament Street, which is full of trim and brightly painted wooden homes with picket fences. As you walk down the street you'll hear the sounds of daily activity floating through the open windows, occasionally a radio station with news, or maybe evangelical songs. You can browse in the general stores and souvenir shops or visit one of the small art galleries that sell original works and prints by local artists. On the left as you walk away from the harbor you'll find the Memorial Sculpture Garden, dedicated to the brave settlers

Pretty as a postcard: picket fences in New Plymouth, Green Turtle Cay.

who founded New Plymouth. A little farther along, on the right, the **Albert Lowe Museum**, in an 18th-century house, is brim full of artifacts and knickknacks, maps, and newspaper articles that tell the story of New Plymouth. Lowe was a sailor and prominent shipbuilder. The house is now owned by Roland Alton Lowe, a descendant of Albert and an acclaimed Bahamian painter; his paintings and prints are sold at the museum. Abaco Gold necklaces, bracelets, and rings—including some with turtle and conch shell motifs—are sold at the Sand Dollar Shoppe on Parliament Street (Tel. 365-4221).

Eleuthera

The longest unbroken island in the Bahamas, slender **Eleuthera** (pronounced "e-LOOTH-ra") extends 100 miles

(160 km) from north to south yet has many stretches that are barely half a mile (1 km) wide. Some of the wildest Bahamian landscapes are to be found on this island that seems to be more in touch with the moods of the sea than other islands are. The rocky outcrops and sometimes towering waves on the east contrast with calm waters and sandy flats on the west. In the northwest a series of cays and sand banks reach out to fill the 60 miles (96 km) or so between Eleuthera and New Providence.

Modern Bahamian history began on this island in 1648 when the Eleutherian Adventurers, led by William Sayle, arrived from Britain and Bermuda and founded their shaky colony. They landed near the site of Governor's Harbour on the middle of the island, but after a period of feuding Sayle and some of his followers moved north to Harbour Island and Spanish Wells. Their descendants still live there today. Although they named the island Eleuthera, you may find that the local people call the island Cigatoo, its old Lucayan name.

Harbour Island, called "Briland" by the locals, sits off the northeastern corner of the main island. You can reach it via a 15-minute ride on a small ferry; taxis from North Eleuthera Airport run reliable service to the docks for a set price per person. The island's main town, **Dunmore Town**, is a cluster of narrow streets lined by clapboard houses festooned with bougainvillea; handsome roosters strut here and there in the undergrowth. Boat building and sugar production used to be the main ways the inhabitants earned a living; rum production also made the town popular with Americans during Prohibition. Now tourism is the major industry.

Bay Street runs along the harbor-front, where you'll find a small straw market—five or six colorful stalls hugging the beach—and the tourist office at the end of the jetty. Wandering around (you can stroll over the entire island in a few hours) you'll find the Loyalist Cottage, a late-18th-century settler's home, as well as several simple churches, including the oldest Anglican church in the Bahamas, St. John's. A number of souvenir shops in the houses have some interesting Bahamian and European gifts.

The beautiful pink sand beach on the Atlantic side of the island is also a big draw. The five miles of sand are a beautiful sight, especially in the early morning or just before sunset when the color reflects more deeply. Any of the several luxury hotels tucked just behind the dunes make a good base for the beach or the delights of the town, only a few minutes' walk away.

Just off the northern tip of Eleuthera is **Spanish Wells**. In the 16th century the Spaniards sank a well here to supply their treasure fleets with fresh water for the long journey back across the Atlantic. The people of Spanish Wells are noted seamen and farmers (they were given land to farm on the main island in the 18th century); many still make their living by fishing for crawfish, grouper, yellowtail, and conch, or by building boats, though the best-known local product is perhaps the wide-brimmed Spanish Wells straw hat. Not as much a tourist resort as Harbour Island, this quiet settlement nevertheless attracts visitors with its beaches, marina, and miles of offshore reef, particularly good for diving. The Spanish Wells Museum (open Mon–Sat 10am–12pm and 1–3pm) records the island's history and culture.

Pink Sands

The fine pink sand found at Harbour Island and all along the east coast of Eleuthera gets its tint from a species of coral protozoans called foraminifers, which are red in color and break down with the action of the water. They add just a hint of color to the golden grains of sand.

This pink-sand beach, framed by the glittering blue of the Atlantic, is the pride of Harbour Island, Eleuthera.

On the northern coast of Eleuthera Island is **Preacher's Cave**, the spot where the original adventurers are said to have been shipwrecked. It is cathedral-like in its dimensions. The settlers wrote their names in charcoal on the walls of the cavern and erected a stone altar for their services (unfortunately the entrance to the cave is now littered with rubbish left by modern travelers). Several deserted beaches nearby, including Preacher's Cay Beach, Bain Bay, and Ridley Head, offer opportunities for solitude or very good close-to-shore snorkeling.

A few miles south of North Eleuthera Airport the island narrows to a rocky ridge just 80 ft (24 m) wide. Over the millennia, an arched hole had been created here by the pounding of the waves of the Atlantic; known as the **Glass Window**, this opening made it possible for sailors on the Exuma Sound to see "through the island" to the Atlantic. The natural bridge that had

Glass Window, where the angry Atlantic pounds its way toward the calm Caribbean.

been formed at the top of the arch collapsed years ago during a hurricane and today you pass over the still dramatic gap from north to central Eleuthera on the man-made Glass Window Bridge. The bridge requires continual maintenance because storms, hurricanes, high winds, and heavy seas take a constant toll; in turbulent weather the Atlantic rises in great waves pushing towards the still, calm Caribbean.

The first settlement after Glass Window Bridge is **Gregory Town**, a pretty hillside community of colorful houses overlooking a tiny harbor. This is the capital of pineapple production in the Bahamas. Try the fresh pies from Thompson's Bakery on the top of a hill east of the harbor. Halfway down the island is **Governor's Harbour**, a photogenic town set on the sheltered eastern coastline. It is a major center for sailors, who come here to stock up on all the essentials, obtain spare parts, and have repairs done.

Windermere Island, just off the east coast, was once the place to be in the Bahamas, but its smart resort hotel is now closed. Jacques Cousteau had a home here and used it as a base for exploring the seas around the other Bahamian islands.

Southern Eleuthera is served by an airport near the little town of **Rock Sound**, which is famed for its blue hole, which Jacques Cousteau spent time investigating. Although it is only half a mile from the Caribbean side of the island, it actually reaches out several miles to the Atlantic Ocean and has yet to be fully explored.

On the Out Islands, use VHF radio. Where there are few telephone lines, it's the way that everyone keeps in touch. Channel 16 is the communal channel that everyone monitors. Call in with your lunch or dinner reservations or your golf-cart rental request and it gets sorted out.

Andros

Andros is the largest island of the Bahamas—at a little over 100 miles (160 km) long and 40 miles (64 km) wide, it's almost four times larger than any other island in the Commonwealth—though much of its territory is covered by uninhabitable mangrove swamp and coral limestone escarpments divided by wide creeks. The island is fringed by miles of shallow sand flats on the west and ringed by coral reef on the east. Perhaps because of its vastness and rugged terrain, Andros became a favorite of the pirate fleets; one of its major settlements is called Morgan's Bluff after the pirate leader Henry Morgan, who is said to have buried treasure on one of the beaches in the area.

In 1821 a group of Seminole Indians left their native Florida and settled on the northern tip of the island. Their descendants still live around the town of **Red Bays**, practicing the skills of basket weaving for which they are greatly admired. Their work, which is of extremely high quality, is said to be so tightly woven that the baskets can hold water.

The family of Neville Chamberlain, the British Prime Minister who attempted to negotiate with Hitler before World War II, created a sisal farm on the island, but the attempt failed miserably.

Andros is famed for its natural attractions: It has the third longest barrier reef in the world, lying just one mile (1½ km) offshore and stretching 140 miles (225 km) down the east coast. This makes it a popular destination with divers who come to explore the tidal shallows, the reef, and the deep reef walls, which plunge 6,000 ft (1,829 m) down into the **Tongue of the Ocean**, the deep passage between Andros and New Providence. Numerous species of sea life flourish at every level and contribute to the abundant variety of diving environments available for all ability levels. Experienced divers also come to explore the numerous so-called "blue holes" that dot the interior of the island. Created by erosion of the limestone rock, these holes have a layer of fresh water that lies on top and tidal sea water below; sea water forced in through countless underground fissures causes their water levels to rise or fall with the tides. Andros is awash with fresh water, which is put to good use: over 6 million gallons are pumped into tankers each day and shipped across to New Providence, where fresh water is much in demand.

Learn how to operate a golf cart—on many small cays this is the easiest way to get around.

The miles of shallow "flats" that meet the mangrove swamps along the west coast are an ideal environment for bonefish, and Andros lays claim to being the Bonefishing Capital of the World. The fishing is extremely challenging, either from boats off the island or by wading in the shallows just offshore. Onshore, Andros is a bird watcher's paradise—hardwood forests of Bahamian mahogany and mangrove and smaller areas of pine offer a varied habitat to over 120 native and migratory species.

Most of the major settlements lie along the eastern side of the island. They are widely scattered, from Congo Town in the south through Andros Town to Nicholls Town in the north. Getting around the island is time consuming and difficult because it is divided by wide creeks, swamps, and lakes, but each of these main settlements is served by an airport.

At Andros Town, known as Fresh Creek to local people, there are a few facilities for visitors and a number of small hotels. One of the most popular Bahamian souvenirs

Another reason to visit Andros! Androsia batik in bright, summery hues.

is produced nearby. Androsia batik—brightly colored cotton fabric with tropical fish, turtle, or fruit motifs—is hand-produced at a small factory just outside the capital. You can watch the patterns being pressed in wax onto the white cotton fabric and view the skeins as they're allowed to dry naturally in the warm Bahamian sun. The finished batik is then used to make clothing and other products in the small factory next door. The products are available in shops all over the Bahamas, but you can save a good deal by buying direct from the factory.

Two's a crowd… Stocking Cay sports a host of sublime beaches, many as deserted as this one.

The Exumas

Running in a 100-mile (160-km) chain directly south of New Providence, the Exumas have a cay for every day of the year, though some of these tiny islands are only a few hundred square feet in size and most are uninhabited. The breathtaking waters surrounding these islands, ranging from turquoise blue to jade green, are a sailor's delight, and numerous yachts can be seen weaving around the sandy shallows and cutting through to deeper water.

The name Exuma is said to be a derivation of the two Lucayan Indian words that had been used for this group of islands, *yumey* and *suma*. The largest Exuma Cays were settled by British Loyalists following the American Revolution. Chief among these was Dennis Rolle, who brought over 100 slaves with him to start a cotton plantation. This venture began to fail after only a few years but Dennis passed the land onto his son

John. In 1834 slavery was abolished and John Rolle freed his slaves and deeded the Rolle land on to them "in commonage" at his death. This allowed only those directly related to the Rolle slaves to farm or build on the inherited land. Today most of the native inhabitants of the Exumas bear the family name Rolle.

The Exumas are divided into three distinct sections: Great Exuma Island, Little Exuma Island, and the Exhuma Cays, which lie north of the main islands. The capital, **George Town**, on Great Exuma Island, is served by regular flights from Nassau and makes the most convenient base for non-sailors. It has a sleepy and laid-back atmosphere and offers a couple of hotels and restaurants. A compact straw and vegetable market sits at the main crossroads. The town lies on the coast at Elizabeth Harbour, a large, sheltered stretch of water that is a popular stopping off point for sailors. The quiet town comes to life every

> **Try a little conch. Not quite as strange as it may sound, conch is a nutritious mollusk loved by all Bahamians, either fresh in a salad, fried in batter, in chowder, or ground and formed into conch "burgers."**

April when it hosts the Family Island Regatta. Thousands of Bahamian working boats fill Elizabeth Harbour, their crews vying for the right to call themselves champion of the regatta.

From George Town you can take the short ferry trip to nearby **Stocking Cay**. The ten-minute journey across the sound (courtesy of the Club Peace and Plenty hotel) takes you to an island of sublime beaches, underwater caves to dive in, and rocky inlets to explore by snorkel. You can find sand dollars and starfish and spot rays and turtles. The few holiday homes do nothing to spoil the natural beauty, and you'll still be able to find a deserted beach in one of the many sheltered bays.

Much of Great Exuma is given over to agricultural production, providing the island New Providence with a lot of its fresh produce. Staples like onions as well as such "exotics" as avocados are grown in the interior. The only other major settlement besides George Town is Rolle Town, once part of the Rolle estate. It is said that the original inhabitants of this town were the family's domestic slaves; the plantation slaves made their home at Rolleville farther north. A number of tombs in Rolle Town date from the earliest days of Loyalist settlement.

A little bridge links Great Exuma with Little Exuma in the south. Until the bridge was opened in 1966 the only way to reach the island was by ferry boat, and the first small settlement on the Little Exuma side is called, appropriately, **The Ferry**. Here you can meet with the "Shark Lady." The first woman to captain a boat in the Family Regatta, Gloria Patience was given her nickname because of the many sharks she has caught. She has created a small museum in her home, the only one of its kind in the Exumas, to document and illustrate the history and lifestyle of the island's people.

Traveling north from George Town you'll pass **Three Sisters Rock**, a formation that lies just offshore from a sandy beach; the three rocks are said to represent three sisters who drowned in the waters here. Gradually the island narrows, and past Rolleville, Great Exuma gives way to the Exuma Cays, a ribbon of small

A hummingbird in action: this may be the most frenetic activity in all the Exumas!

islands of which only four are inhabited. **Stanial Cay** offers accommodation as well as yachting supplies. It also has an airfield with regular service from Fort Lauderdale on the Florida coast. These cays are home to the endangered iguana along with numerous rare plant species. A 22-mile (35-km) stretch north of Conch Cut has been protected for future generations by the creation of the **Exuma Cays Land and Sea Park**, 175 sq miles (453 sq km) of land and sea that includes some of the best yet most remote beaches in the Bahamas. The park is only accessible by

Hemingway's house, Bimini; the great writer was one of many fans of the tiny isles.

boat—except for the occasional powerboats bringing passengers over from Nassau for a day of snorkeling and picnics on the beach, the only sounds you'll hear will be the wind whipping through the sails of yachts anchored offshore.

Bimini

Two tiny islands only 9 sq miles (23 sq km) in total area, North and South Bimini lie just 50 miles (80 km) east of Miami in the midst of some of the best sport fishing waters in the world. Both have had an illustrious list of admirers. Ponce de Leon searched for the Fountain of Youth here. Ernest Hemingway spent a lot of time fishing and writing here—photographs of

North and South Bimini boast some of the best sport fishing waters in the world.

this prominent visitor still adorn the walls of the Compleat Angler Hotel, where he wrote *To Have and Have Not*. American politician Adam Clayton Powell, who was regularly seen at the marina of Alice Town, the major settlement, helped raise the profile of the place in the eyes of Americans. The islands flourished during the years of American Prohibition, when many came here to enjoy a shot or two of hard liquor.

Alice Town with its bars and hotels is still the center of the action. A series of fishing competitions make up a "season" for the rich, bright, and beautiful, who descend to fish during the day and enjoy the lively social scene after dark. Although Bimini does not have the casinos and stage shows of Nassau and Grand Bahama, the Hemingway legacy seems to keep the bars along the quay in a perpetual state of jovial excess. Off-shore in only 15 ft (4½ m) of water, lies the famed ancient roadway said to be part of the lost city of Atlantis.

The Berry Islands

This group of islands north of Andros and New Providence, only 12 sq miles (4½ sq km) in all, are known as the "fish-bowl of the Bahamas" because of the rich seas around them. They are a paradise for fishermen, divers, and snorkelers. Scattered across some of the prettiest seas in the Bahamas, with shallow sand banks and a thousand translucent hues of green and blue, these cays can be seen quite clearly from the air on flights from Florida. They can also be explored by boat; anchoring in the sheltered waters provides outstanding opportunities for swimming and snorkeling.

Two of the Berry Islands offer tourist facilities. **Chub Cay**, nearest to Nassau, is a favored sport-fishing resort—anglers sail out from here to the northern tip of the Tongue of the Ocean to catch marlin. Scuba divers and snorkelers enjoy the shallow reefs close to the island. The shallow coral reef off Mamma Rhoda Rock, a brief motorboat ride from Chub Cay marina, is an outstanding experience. Great Harbour Cay, covered with silver-top palms and sea grape, is a pretty island with a number of marvelous beaches. At the impressive marina, yachtsmen—many visiting from the Florida coast—park in slips beneath their townhouses.

Cat Island

Cat Islanders can still be said to be living a little in the past. For one thing, they dispute nearby San Salvador's claim to be the landing place of Columbus; they still feel, as archaeologists and historians used to, that the explorer first made landfall on their island. The Cat Islanders also retain a powerful attach-

Scuba divers take to the waters of San Salvador where reef diving is spectacular.

ment to *obeah,* the world of spirits and natural healing.

The island itself also has peculiarities that separate it from other Bahamian Islands. It is the most undulating of the islands; one could even call it hilly, with the highest point of land in the Commonwealth, Mount Alvernia, rising to the heady heights of 216 ft (66 m) above sea level.

Many visitors come to this island, named after an English sea captain called Catt, for its beautiful quiet beaches. Fernandez Bay, with its arc of fine sand on the protected western side of the island, is said to be the finest in the Bahamas, and the nearby beach at Old Bight is not far behind in terms of beauty. Though you can't go wrong anywhere on the western coast.

Mount Alvernia, in the center of the island, is not far from the airfield at New Bight. This settlement originally served as a hermitage for Father Jerome, an Anglican missionary who had converted to Catholicism and become an influential churchman on the Out Islands, responsible for the erection of a number of Catholic Churches. Father Jerome built a small Hermitage on the heights of Mount Alvernia that you'll see as you reach the summit (a 15-minute walk from a rudimentary car park); the missionary was buried in a small hilltop cave here upon his death in 1956 at the age of 80. A more recent famous Cat Islander is the actor Sidney Poitier, who was born in Arthur's Town in the north. He is now non-resident Bahamian Ambassador to Japan.

San Salvador

This tiny patch of land, 63 sq miles in area, is at the center of a momentous turning point in history, for it was here that Christopher Columbus first made landfall in the New World, on 12 October 1492. One can only imagine the relief of his crew, and perhaps Columbus's own sense of satisfaction that his theories had proved to be correct (though not entirely, since he assumed he had found the Indian subcontinent).

Around the shoreline of San Salvador are four separate places that are purported to be the site of Columbus's landing.

This cross commemorates Columbus's arrival at the "New World," landing at San Salvador.

No one will ever know for sure, of course, but the competition continues. After the Spaniards went on to other islands in the Caribbean, the island became a base for English pirate John Watling; indeed until 1926 it was known as Watling's Island.

The interior of San Salvador is dotted with lakes; there is a great deal of marshy land and only one major road. **Cockburn Town** (pronounced "KOE-burn") is the capital. Pride of place in the town goes to the small jail found by the main coast road. It's now a museum because, as one resident said, "we don't have no need for no jail." (The opening hours are irregular.)

The main road leads around the circumference of the island. Heading south from Cockburn Town you'll first come to Long Bay, the "official" site of Columbus's landing. It is marked by a plain white cross that sits bright and stark against the azure-blue ocean on the seaward side of the road.

Stella Maris Beach, Long Island. When Columbus sighted this island, he declared it the most beautiful he'd ever seen.

The area has been designated as **Landfall Park**. Another monument, to the 1968 Olympics in Mexico, sits a little way from the cross. This depiction of the Olympic rings on a circular plinth is here because the Olympic flame was brought to San Salvador on its way to Mexico.

At the northeastern corner of the island is **Dixon Hill Lighthouse**. Built in 1856 but improved in subsequent years, it is called the last hand-operated kerosene-powered lighthouse in the Bahamas. Its beam can be seen for some 20 miles (32 km).

San Salvador has developed a reputation as one of the best places in the Bahamas for reef wall diving. The walls off the western coast are almost vertical in places, and schools of hammerheads can be seen regularly in the pristine waters. The island has only two hotels, but a well-organized dive center runs a professional program for those who want to explore the seas off the island.

Long Island

When Columbus sighted this island he stated that it was the most beautiful that he had ever seen. He named it Fernandina in honor of the King of Spain, but the English called it Long Island because of its appearance — 66 miles (106 km) long and no more than 4 miles (6½ km) in width.

The Spaniards wiped out the population of Lucayan Indians who lived here, and the island remained unpopulated for over 200 years, until it was settled by a number of Loyalist families from the American colonies. They attempted to grow cotton in the thin layer of soil but were unsuccessful, and at the announcement of emancipation they abandoned the island, leaving their slaves behind.

Today excitement centers on the resort of **Stella Maris** in the north, which was developed in the 1960s by a group of German businessmen. One of the premier diving sites in the

Bahamas, the resort was one of the first to develop shark-feeding programs at Shark Reef, famous feeding grounds of these formidable creatures. The waters sweep over dozens of pretty beaches, and rocky outcrops provide ideal areas for snorkeling. The finest beach is at the very northern tip of the island— Cape Santa Maria (named by Columbus after his own ship) is a vast empty expanse of yellow sand and blue sea.

Long Island's one main road runs like a backbone down its length. This highway creates an artificial divide between the two very different coastlines. In the east, the Atlantic Ocean crashes against cliffs of coral. In the west, the gentle seas lap shallow sand banks that stretch towards the southern Exumas.

Traveling south from Stella Maris you'll pass uninhabited mangrove swamps on the way to the small town of Simms, an unhurried old settlement known for its distinctive straw-work, which craftswomen are delighted to show visitors. At **Deadman's Cay** you'll find an extensive cave system with faded Lucayan rock drawings. After passing small pineapple and banana plantations, you'll reach attractive **Clarence Town**, with its two large churches—one Anglican, the other Roman Catholic—built by Cat Island hermit architect Father Jerome. The blue hole at nearby **Turtle Cove**, a half-mile walk from the road over rough terrain, provides a memorable diving experience, though it's interesting even from the rim. The hole is about 80 yards (73 m) across and at least 600 ft (183 m) deep; you'll sometimes see large turtles and tarpon in the waters.

Crooked Island and Acklins Island

These two islands lie 225 miles (360 km) south of Nassau and are totally off the beaten path for most tourists today, though they were often visited during the age of steam ships. Columbus described them as "the fragrant islands" after the smell of cascarilla, an indigenous tree; the bark is a major ingredient in perfumes, medicines, and in the Italian aperitif Campari. The **Ocean Den** marine cave system in the Bight of Acklins is one of the most impressive in the Bahamas. The totally unspoiled long sandy beaches provide a rich environment for birds and animal life. The area to the west of the two islands is a shallow sheltered lagoon where many small cays offer protection to a rare species of iguana.

Crooked Island has challenging diving sites, particularly along the reef wall off its northern shore line. Aklins has good bonefish flats with virgin fish shoals, though there are few tourist facilities and as yet no major plans to expand facilities.

Mayaguana Island

This island 75 miles (120 km) east of Acklins Island, is perhaps the least visited and least developed of all the inhabited Bahamas islands. It has few telephones and electric power is only a recent development. The settlement of Pirates Well harks back to the days when it was a safe outpost for ruthless gangs, but today's population makes a living from fishing and farming.

Inagua

Great Inagua and Little Inagua Islands are the most southerly of the Bahamas—Great Inagua lies just 50 miles (80 km) from the coast of Cuba. The primary sources of employment are fishing and salt collection; over 1 million tons of salt are exported each year. There are few tourist facilities here, and both islands are natural and unspoiled, hosting many rare forms of wildlife. **Inagua National Park** on Great Inagua has the largest breeding colony of the West Indian Flamingo left in the world; the population of over 60,000 is found around Lake Windsor and Lake Rosa in the interior of the island. The park also supports a turtle-breeding ground and provides a home to wild boar and wild donkeys.

EXCURSIONS OUTSIDE THE BAHAMAS
Greater Miami

Miami is America's youngest big city. Development began only in 1896, when the Florida East Coast railroad was extended to the region. In the 1920s the region began to attract wealthy Americans from the north, who came to escape the cold winters. Since Castro's revolution in Cuba greater Miami has welcomed millions of Cuban and other Latin American settlers. The area has strong trading links with South and Central America and the Caribbean. Today cruise ships, yachts, fishing boats, and freighters keep the waterfront humming while traffic never ceases along the futuristic network of expressways; and Miami's sprawling international airport is one of the busiest in the US.

Miami is alive with energy. A fusion of styles has put the city at the forefront of American art, dance, music, and cuisine. Downtown, the Bayside shopping center has revitalized the docks area. Chain stores and craft stalls sit alongside cafés and bars, and on weekends there's live music on stage at the center's main plaza.

The city's first language is in fact Spanish; more than one-third of the inhabitants are Hispanic, many of whom live in **Little Havana**, west of downtown. Though many Cubans have now moved on to wealthier neighborhoods this city-within-a-city full of small shops, cafés, and restaurants still has the flavor of the old life. Watch the men play dominos in Maximo Gomez Park on SW 8th Street—Calle Ocho—and listen to their stories of the old days.

To the southwest of downtown is **Coral Gables**, discreet retreat of the rich and very rich, and full of touches of old Spanish architecture. Look for beautiful Columbus Boulevard, with its arched canopy of spectacular banyan trees.

Waterways at the back of the houses lead out to the sea and the intercoastal waterways that surround the city.

In fashionable **Coconut Grove**, one of the oldest parts of Greater Miami, a shopping and entertainment center attracts visitors and locals alike. The surrounding streets have pretty boutiques that cater to the needs of the wealthy inhabitants. Bahamian timber schooner laborers are given credit for settling Coconut Grove, where today the prices of the most expensive condominiums run into hundreds of thousands of dollars.

South of metropolitan Miami, you'll see hundreds of colorful parrots, macaws, flamingoes, and other tropical birds in the rain forest foliage of Parrot Jungle. Another park where you can meet the animals is Monkey Jungle. Metrozoo, a cageless facility, displays animals compatible with the south Florida climate.

Vizcaya, an Italianate mansion set in 10 acres (24 hectares) of formal gardens by the water's edge, is now a museum with 70 rooms full of treasures. One of the first Miami millionaires, James Deering, hired a huge team of workmen to construct the house in 1916. See the breakwater offshore, in the form of Cleopatra's barge.

Take the Rickenbacker Causeway from Miami to Key

Ocean Drive, South Beach, where people-watching is the prime pastime.

Biscayne to get to one of Miami's star attractions, the 60-acre (148-hectare) **Seaquarium**. You'll see dozens of exotic creatures from the ocean depths. Watch them being fed in the gigantic aquarium tanks, then join up with the crowd outside to see one of the shows. The most spectacular of them features a 9,500-pound (4,318-kg) killer whale who leaps gracefully more than 20 ft (6 m) out of the water, only to fall back again in a thunderous crescendo of dazzling spray.

From Downtown Miami take the MacArthur Causeway east to Miami Beach and the wonderful **Art Deco District** of **South Beach**, or "SoBe," as the locals call it. Many of the hotels and public buildings were built in the boom period of the 1920s and had been left to decay as Miami spread to the west and other areas became more popular. Then in the 1980s, as developers began to regain interest in the area, a group of architects began a campaign to save the Art Deco masterpieces, and South Beach was reborn. Today it is one of the most fashionable places on earth: supermodels and film stars mix with ordinary folks at the bars, restaurants, and hip

The Rocket Garden Display at the world-famous John F. Kennedy Space Center.

boutiques. The Art Deco District has been given a thorough facelift and the colorful, imposing buildings now shine just as they did in their first heyday. This is prime people-watching territory, because on South Beach, particularly along Ocean Drive, just about anything goes, and the action carries on well into the night. At any time of day, it's worth strolling along Lincoln Road, a pedestrian zone lined with street-side cafés and collectibles shops.

Port Canaveral and Orlando

Many cruises to the Bahamas depart from Port Canaveral on Florida's east coast, about halfway up the peninsula. This is an ideal jumping off point for a number of attractions of worldwide fame—the pleasures of Orlando and Walt Disney World and other theme parks are only 50 minutes away. Even closer, just 20 minutes away from the cruise port, is Cape Canaveral and the Kennedy Space Center.

Kennedy Space Center

On Cape Canaveral stands one of the most advanced complexes of technological gadgetry anywhere—the **John F. Kennedy Space Center**. Spread over 220 sq miles (570 sq km), the vast base is an engineer's dream-come-true. The visitors center has a comprehensive collection of lunar modules, rockets, and space shuttle and skylab hardware; at the IMAX cinema, which runs almost continuously throughout the day, you can watch fantastic documentaries of launches, flights, and space walks.

Guided bus tours take you to the mammoth vehicle-assembly building (so huge that it is said clouds sometimes form inside) and to other fascinating displays of space technology in the National Aeronautics and Space Administration Museum. You may be lucky enough to visit on a launch day—earth satellites, space probes, and other research equipment are routinely launched from the Cape. Admission to the Center is free, but there is a charge for IMAX films and the guided tour.

Walt Disney World

They call it the "happiest place on earth," which may be why more visitors now come here than to any other single attraction anywhere. Surprisingly, four of every five are adults. Disney World is styled as the most complete vacation destination in existence, offering sports, nightlife, sightseeing, shopping, camping, hotels, and restaurants all connected by an extensive, easy-to-use transportation network.

The heart of the complex is the 100-acre (40-hectare) **Magic Kingdom**, where it's easy to confuse who's real and who's artificial. This is where the park began and where you can meet all your favorite Disney characters—you'll be able to shake hands with Mickey and get a hug from Goofy. The park has seven sections, including Main Street, USA, with its re-creation of turn-of-the-century America facing the much photographed Cinderella Castle. For a gentle overview of the entire Magic Kingdom, try the aerial tramway at dusk as the lights are coming on.

Out of Walt Disney's last dream of an Experimental Prototype Community of Tomorrow grew **EPCOT Center**, just south of the Magic Kingdom. This multimedia extravaganza's projection of our planet's past and future has all the high-tech displays and virtual-reality of your dreams. Take a ride through the human body, or dash around the world in an afternoon as you step into re-creations of 11 countries.

Disney's Animal Kingdom takes you on a journey from the days of the dinosaurs to the present time. Imaginative state-of-the-art graphics and effects have been used to bring extinct creatures to life, and a large safari park allows you to view live animals in "almost" natural surroundings.

The Disney Magic at Port Canaveral. The port is a popular departure point for cruises to the Bahamas.

Walt Disney World also brings the classic films and characters to life at **Disney–MGM Studios**. With stunt spectaculars and re-creations of movie sets, this attraction shows how the finished films and animations you see on screen are created.

With all of these attractions plus three Water Parks, the Disney Quest Interactive games areas, Pleasure Island, Discovery Island, and the Wide World of Sports complex, there is enough activity to fill weeks of time for even the most energetic children, or adults.

Disney World is about 20 miles southwest of Orlando off Interstate Highway 4. It is open daily, and far into the night at peak periods. For information on the latest opening times, ticket prices, and information, call (407) 824-4321.

Disney Cruises

Disney Cruises run from Port Canaveral, stop at Nassau for a day, and then move on to Disney's private Bahamian hideaway, "Castaway Cay," for days of fun and relaxation. Cruises can be combined in packages that include time at Walt Disney World theme park and a Disney hotel within the park.

Sea World of Florida

A 7,000-pound (3,175-kg) killer whale is the astonishing main attraction at this exciting marine park. The genial black-and-white monster, named Shamu, leaps out of the water, stands on his head waving his enormous tail, lets handlers ride him, and nods his head to questions. Shamu is nearly 22 ft (6½ m) long, eats 200 pounds (90 kg) of food and 50 vitamin pills a day. During a day at the park you can also watch a splendid dolphin ballet, cheer for sea lions playing volleyball, or view seals and penguins frolicking in their tanks. Children especially enjoy having a chance to feed the animals.

Sea World, 12 miles (19 km) southwest of Orlando at I-4 and the Bee Line Expressway, is minutes away from Disney World. It's open daily, and the admission charge covers all shows. For information call (407) 351-3600.

Universal Studios Florida

This theme park where you can "ride the movies" is a huge complex of futuristic and computerized rides based on movie themes. Come face to face with Jaws or ride out a Twister. It feels as if you're really part of the action as your carriage jolts around corners and flames lick close to your seat (all carefully choreographed for utmost safety). Enjoy the fun of the Nickelodeon Studios, where kids programming takes center stage. There are parades and stunt spectaculars and plenty of places to eat. Universal Studios is located off I-4; take exits 29 or 30B.

Orlando Flextickets offer a combination ticket for Sea World, Universal Studios, and the Wet-and-Wild water complex in Orlando; for details call 800-224-3838 of consult the Universal Studios' website, <www.usf.com>.

WHAT TO DO

SHOPPING

What to Buy

Crafts. Bahamians have always had to fend for themselves, and this resourcefulness has led them to become proficient at a number of practical handicrafts, many of which make beautiful souvenirs. **Straw goods** are the most ubiquitous. The Seminole Indians of Red Bay on Andros are said to produce the finest work on the Bahamas, though each island has its own individual patterns and differences in style. It is still possible to watch the women at work on the islands of Andros and at George Town on Exuma. Straw work can be bought from small workshops in people's homes or from the better quality straw vendors in Nassau. Prices can be high, but even small bowls make beautiful and practical reminders of your trip. The handmade pieces are likely to become rare within a couple of generations, because so few young Bahamian women are now taking up the craft. Be aware that much of the straw work, par-

Hats, baskets, bags, and bowls… finely crafted straw goods abound.

ticularly the mass-market goods like hats and bags, is not made in the Bahamas but in Taiwan and China. If you want to be sure of getting genuine Bahamian straw work, buy from places such as The Plait Lady, who has a shop on Bay Street in Nassau; you'll have to pay a little more but you'll be sure you're getting an authentic handmade work of art.

Paintings and art work with scenes of everyday life also make beautiful mementos. The work of a number of artists, including Alton Lowe and Eddie Minnis, is becoming very collectable and prices can be high. On the other end of the scale, street art, including things like driftwood paintings, can be fun and much more affordable.

Wood carvings are made from a variety of native trees. Some of the best are made from the *lignum vitae,* the Bahamian national tree, and from the wild tamarind. The carvings come in a bewildering variety, though animal and fish motifs seem to predominate. Always check a piece thoroughly before you buy as they are vary in quality. Don't buy wood if it looks green—this usually means the wood has not been allowed to season, and it may split as it dries.

Seashells and sponges can be found in every market and souvenir shop in the Bahamas. They make beautiful, natural souvenirs, but some may come from protected species. Do not buy coral or turtle products as this is illegal and only encourages further damage to these delicate and rare forms of sea life.

Clothing. If you like, you could take an empty bag and buy your holiday wardrobe when you arrive in the Bahamas. Many of the shops on Bay Street, at the International Bazaar, and the Port Lucaya Market Place offer beachwear and T-shirts galore. Sarongs, printed dresses, and shirts in light fabrics are sold in almost every craft stall in the straw markets. Light-cotton Androsia clothing, made on Andros, is perfect for the Bahamian climate; you'll find these items all over the Bahamas.

This Japanese welcome gate invites you into Freeport's International Bazaar, where you can shop around the world.

Straw hats, which will protect you from the strong sun and save you from a wrinkle or two, are abundant and inexpensive. You'll be able to choose from styles ranging from the understated to the extremely flamboyant.

Duty-free luxury goods. Both New Providence and Grand Bahama have a good range of luxury duty-free goods for sale. The shops tend to be clustered together, which makes it easy to compare prices and quality before you buy; in Nassau you'll find them on Bay Street and in the International Bazaar, and in the Port Lucaya Market on Grand Bahama. Things to keep an eye out for include gold and silver jewelry and such gem stones as diamonds, sapphires, and emeralds set in gold from Christian Dior and other leading designers. Abaco Gold is a range of jewelry designed and sold only in the Bahamas

Calendar of Events

Each island in the Bahamas hosts a variety of fêtes, fishing competitions, golf tournaments, and other events throughout the year. Check with the Ministry of Tourism when you arrive to find out what's happening during your stay. Here is a list of the major events held throughout the Commonwealth.

January *Junkanoo.* A huge costume parade at 1am New Year's Day is one of the highlights of the annual Bahamian-style carnival that starts on 26 December; street parties are held in Nassau and on several Out Islands.

February *Valentine Massacre Regatta.* Two days of racing and on-shore activities at Montegu Bay, New Providence (Tel. 394-0445 for details).

March *National Arts Festival, Nassau.* March to May. Features art, dance, and drama.

April *The Family Regatta.* George Town in the Exumas comes alive with working boats and tourist boats, street parties and parades (Tel. 336-2430).

May *Long Island Regatta, Salt Pond, Long Island.*

June *The Goombay Summer Festival.* A four-month celebration with events daily. Eleuthera Pineapple Festival, Gregory Town, Eleuthera. Recipe contests, sporting competitions, and street parades.

July *Independence Day.* The 10th of July is celebrated with street parties and fireworks displays. Abaco Regatta, Abaco Island.

August *Emancipation Day.* The first Monday in August commemorates the Emancipation of the Bahamian slaves. A Junkanoo parade starts at 4am at Fox Hill. Fun events happen throughout the day.

September *Angling Tournament, Bimini Big Game Fishing Club.* Two tournaments early and late in the month draw sports fishermen from the US and the Caribbean (Tel. 347-3529).

October *Discovery Day.* The 12th is celebrated with lively street parties, expecially on San Salvador.

December *Junkanoo.* This annual island-wide festival kicks off on Boxing Day (26 Dec).

and unusual pieces such as rare gold and silver coins brought from treasure found on the seabed, and mounted in gold to be worn as pendants or brooches. If it's time for a new timepiece, you can choose from a comprehensive range of watches by names such as Rolex, Breitling, and Tag Hauer. Fragrances from around the world, fine crystal, and European leather goods are also on display in most of the shops.

Duty-free shops will make claims that they save you 30–40 percent on prices you'd pay back home, but this is not universally true, and it's always important to so some research on prices in your hometown before you go. Some goods are only slightly cheaper than back home; doing a little homework before hand will help you sniff out the "real" bargains.

Rum. Bacardi and other Caribbean brands, like Appletons of Jamaica, and almost all international brands of liquor can be found at good prices. Look out for coconut rum and other fruit rums—there's a tremendous variety.

Where to Shop

Bay Street in Nassau and the **International Bazaar** in Freeport are the major tourist shopping areas, but Out Islanders often sell hand-crafted items, and some resorts have boutiques.

Stores are generally open 9am–5pm, and are closed Sundays, holidays, and possibly Thursday, Friday, or Saturday afternoon. The Nassau and Freeport straw markets are open every day and even sometimes after dark. Shops will often mail your purchases home for you.

Bargaining at outdoor stalls, something of a tourist pastime for the straw ladies, might get you a discount. But don't bother trying in regular stores where you pay the posted price. There is no sales tax in the Bahamas.

Here are some of the most dependable shops on the Out Islands: In Hope Town, Water's Edge Studios offers wood

Put that in writing! This Hope Town store goes the extra mile—or is this a tourist trap?

carvings by Russ Ervin, and Island Gallery stocks selected handicrafts and souvenirs. Island Made Gift Shop in Gregory Town (Eleuthera; Tel. 335-5369) has a good supply of Bahamian gifts and crafts. Reliable spots to shop for Abaco Gold are Green Turtle Cay and Marsh Harbour.

SPORTS

The Bahamas Sports and Aviation Information Centre provides complete information about sports facilities in the Bahamas. Call them toll-free at 800-32-SPORT (within the US only) or at 305-932-0051, or write for information to 19495 Biscayne Boulevard, Suite 809, Aventura, Florida 33180, USA.

Water Sports

Wind surfing. With its many shallow lagoons, the Bahamas is a great place for wind surfing. Most large hotels have boards for rent. Para-sailing (soaring overhead in a parachute harness pulled by a speedboat) is also available in New Providence

(Cable Beach and Paradise Island) and Grand Bahama (Lucaya), but make sure you're fully insured before taking to the air—many policies exclude this popular activity. Sea Sports at the Nassau Marriott Resort on Cable Beach has a full compliment of water-sport equipment for rent (Tel. 327-6200).

Diving and snorkeling. Opportunities for diving and snorkeling in the Bahamas are almost unrivaled in terms of both the quality of the experience and the variety of stunning habitats. The area's clear waters and numerous coral reefs and rocky outcrops offer an ideal environment for hundreds of species of fish, as well as turtles, dolphins, and, yes, sharks. A number of dive centers offer transport to the sites along with the assistance of experienced and qualified dive masters. The two main centers on Nassau and Grand Bahama are Nassau Scuba Centre (Tel. 362-1964; fax 362-1198; US Tel. (954) 462-3400; US fax (954) 462-4100; website <http://www.nassau-scuba-centre.com,)> and UNEXSO (Tel. 373-1244; fax 373-8956; US Tel. (954) 351-9889; US fax (954) 351-9740). Both of these companies also run trips to Andros, Eleuthera, and Exuma. You'll also find diving and snorkeling opportunities on the main islands of New Providence and Grand Bahama. And there are special places around the Out Islands that offer exceptional experiences, though not much lively entertainment out of the water. Here is a list of particularly exciting sites:

New Providence. Thunderball and Canonball reefs. Just off the coast of Rose Island and named for the James Bond films that were filmed here; the coral formations are impressive and large fish such as grouper are numerous.

Grand Bahama. Theo's Wreck. The MV Island Cement was deliberately sunk in 1982 to create an artificial dive site, though the creatures that inhabit the area don't seem to be bothered by the man-made skeleton. Moray eels and thousands of angel fish now live among the coral and sponges.

*Water worship: at **Andros** (above) and at **Coral Rose Beach, Harbour Island**.*

Andros. The barrier reef here is the third longest in the world. At 60 ft (20 m) below the surface, it is for divers only, though snorkelers can splash around in the shallow coastal areas, which are also rich in sea life. Spectacular large fish and sharks are usually sighted here at the "Tongue of the Ocean," which in some places lies only 120 ft (40 m) offshore but drops an amazing 6000 ft (2000 m) to the ocean trench. There are also several "blue holes"—vivid blue ocean holes, some with mazes of tunnels and caves—to be explored. Small Hope Bay Lodge on Andros offers diving vacations (Tel. 368-2014; fax 368-2015).

Bimini. At Paradise Point you can explore the formations that are said to be the lost city of Atlantis. Contact Bill and Nowddla Keefe's Bimini Undersea for information on ex-

cursions (Tel. 347-3089; fax 652-9148; US Tel. (305) 653-5572; US fax (305) 652-9148).

San Salvador. Because the reef wall here lies only 40 ft (15 m) below the surface, this site is much more accessible for less experienced divers than the Andros reef. It's said to be a great place to see groups of hammerhead sharks as well as turtles and huge rays. Contact Riding Rock Inn for information on diving (Tel. 331-2631; fax 331-2020; US Tel. (954) 359-8353; US fax (954) 359-8254).

Long Island. Shark Reef near Stella Maris is the most famous area in the islands for close encounters with that most feared aquatic creature. Here you can watch the "feeding frenzy" of sharks from close quarters. There are also pristine reef walls off Conception Island and Rum Cay. Contact the

Stella Maris Resort (Tel. 338-2050; fax 338-2052; US Tel. (954) 359-8236; US fax (954) 359-8238).

The Abacos. The Cathedral, west of Guana Cay, is a huge cave lit with sunlight streaming through holes in the ceiling; The large entrance makes it relatively safe for novice divers. Walkers Cay's shark-feeding program allows divers to watch large groups of sharks fight over a frozen fish "chumsickle" (buckets of fish parts frozen into a block that thaws in the warm water, releasing the fish slowly to prolong the feeding). Contact Walkers Cay Undersea Adventures (Tel. 352-1252; fax 353-1339; US Tel. (954) 462-3400; US fax (954) 462-4100).

The Exumas. Pick almost any island or islet here for tremendous possibilities. Fast power boats from Nassau whisk visitors on day trips to enjoy the area. The Blue Holes around Stocking Island attract varied fish life. Contact Exuma Fantasea for more information (Tel. and fax 336-2483).

Remember to take your dive certificate along—you won't be allowed to rent equipment and dive unless you can prove your competence.

If you want to learn to dive in the Bahamas, or if you want to upgrade your skills, you can contact one of the many excellent dive centers that offer training for all levels. All centers are affiliated with one of the major certifying bodies, PADI (Professional Association of Diving Instructors) being the most common. The basic qualification, the Open Water certificate, takes five days to complete. Once you have this, you'll be allowed to dive with an instructor to a depth of 60 ft (18 m), which opens up many dive sites in the Bahamas to you.

Many centers also offer an introductory session commonly known as the "Discover Scuba Programme." This involves a morning or afternoon of theory and swimming-pool work that will give you the chance to try out the basic techniques. Many large hotels offer this "taster" to their guests.

Sport fishing. The waters around the islands and cays teem with fish, and the Bahamas also happen to be on the migration routes of many species. This all adds up to make the Bahamas one of the world's greatest territories for game fishing. The Commonwealth currently holds world records for several species of fish. Sport fishing—that is, catching fish and returning them to the water—is hugely popular, and you can charter fishing boats by the half-day, full day, or week on almost every one of the main islands. The local guides are especially experienced and helpful. The Bimini Islands have been the capital of sport fishing for decades; here you'll find hundreds of huge boats lining the marinas waiting to be taken out into the teeming waters. (Ernest Hemingway led the way here.) Bonefishing is also big business around the islands. Large, strong inedible fish that frequent the shallows and sand flats, bonefish are said to be the most difficult species in the

Best Months for Fish

The months given below are the very best times (rated "excellent") to go after that particular fish. In other months the rating for the fish in question ranges from only "average" to "good."

Barracuda	June–August
Blue Marlin	May–June
Bonefish	Good to excellent year-round
Grouper	April–September
Kingfish	Good all year
Sailfish	April
Shark	April–June
Snapper	April–September
Swordfish	June–September
Tuna (3 species)	March–July
Wahoo	November–March
White Marlin	May

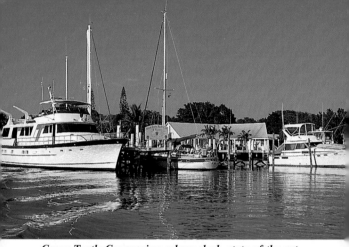

Green Turtle Cay marina, where sleek, state-of-the-art boats are a dime a dozen.

world to catch. Andros has long claimed to be the "bonefishing capital of the world," but other Bahamian islands are vying for its crown. Bimini offers exciting opportunities and the Exumas, North Eleuthera, and San Salvador are all throwing their gloves into the ring. Acklins Island is said to be surrounded by virgin water for anglers—the fish are still unaware of the lure or the fly, though tourist facilities are limited here.

You have to move out to the deep-water sounds, however, to get to the big fish such as marlin, sailfish, and tuna. The "Tongue of the Ocean," especially where it narrows between Andros and New Providence, and Exuma Sound around Cat Island are well loved by the knowledgeable.

As a general rule, the larger and more populous islands have the newer and better boats for rent. Prices vary, but a full day's charter of a boat and crew averages $400–$500. Half-day rentals are also available. Contact one of the following for additional information: Days Catch Charter, Abaco (Tel. 809/336-0059); Coopers Charter Service, George Town, Exuma (Tel. 809/336-2711); or Peace and Plenty Bonefish Lodge, George Town, Exuma (Tel. 345-5555; fax 345-5556). The Andros Island Bonefishing Lodge is a prime center for bonefishing expeditions (Tel. 368-5167; fax 368-2026).

Sailing. With hundreds of unpopulated islands and dozens of empty beaches surrounded by dozens of shallow channels and sounds the Bahamas are paradise for sailors. Safe harbors with superb facilities, cozy coves for a night alone, and the possibility of making short hops to a different port every night allow sailors to experience all the different atmospheres of the various islands.

On many of the islands, renting a boat is as easy as renting a car is in other destinations—especially on the more populated Out Islands. Rentals can vary from small runabouts that will get you around the harbor and the coastal shallows to large sailing yachts and motor launches for inter-island expeditions. Rates vary enormously. To make more of a stay in the Abacos or Exumas, where there are many outlaying cays, you can rent a 18-ft (5½-m) boat with small outboard motor for around $80 per day. Larger vessels come with a crew and/or guide; if you sail your own boat, you can take advantage of the services of a local guide to take you to fishing, snorkeling, or dive sites.

The Abacos are most popular spot for sailing, primarily because of the many sheltered harbors and the many islands and cays that you can reach without having to go outside of the reefs and into ocean waters. If you want to get out and see a lot of boats without doing any sailing, head to the Bahamas during the Regattas, when boats crowd the harbors and the little towns are full of yachtsmen. Listen to the stories of heroic deeds in the bars and enjoy the wonderful views of masts filling the skies.

For information about sailing rentals contact The Moorings (Tel. 367-4000; fax 367-4004; website <http://www.moorings.com>). Smaller boats for local jaunts can be rented at Sea Horse Boat Rentals, Marsh Harbour, Abacos (Tel. 367-2513; fax 367-2516; website <http://www.sea-horse.com>. Nassau Yacht Haven also has sailboats for rent (Tel. 393-8173).

Flying

For qualified pilots the Bahamas offers one of the ultimate flying experiences. There are numerous small airfields on the outlying islands, and flying between the islands is relatively safe, with short transfers. Looking down at the shallow waters and deep ocean trenches is perhaps the only way to truly appreciate the beauty of the shifting sand banks and tranquil remote islands. Private pilots can rent aircraft at Nassau and

If you need some time out from the beach, the Bahamas has its share of green. Golfers tee off, here on Grand Bahama.

Grand Bahama Aero Clubs; it's also relatively simple to rent an aircraft in Florida for the short hop into the Bahamas.

Golf

The Bahamas has a number of PGA-level courses. Grand Bahama has the well tended Lucaya Golf and Country Club (Tel. 373-1066), and the Bahamas Princess Golf and Country Club, part of the Bahamas Princess Complex at Freeport, has two courses (Tel. 352-6721) both designed by Dick Wilson. New Providence has Paradise Island Golf Club (Tel. 363-3925) and one at Cable Beach (Tel. 327-6000). On Abaco Island, Treasure Beach has an 18-hole course (Tel. 365-8045).

Boat Tours

If you don't sail yourself, this is a great way to see the Bahamas from the water. Even if you can't get out to some of the Out Islands, such as the Exumas, you can sail out to one of the cays near Nassau to get a feel for the atmosphere of the more remote parts of the Bahamas. Top Sail Yacht Cruises takes small parties from the British Colonial Beach Dock to places like Rose Island (Tel. 393-0820). Majestic Tours, at Prince George Dock, has the largest boats (Tel. 322-2606). On Grand Bahama, Superior Watersports offers daily cruises (Tel. 373-7863).

NIGHTLIFE

Your evening's entertainment depends on the island on which you find yourself. On many of the Out Islands fun centers around having dinner and a couple of drinks in the local bar, finishing a few pages of the book you brought, watching the stars, or planning the next day's diving or sailing. On Nassau and Grand Bahama, however, there's plenty to keep you occupied until the morning hours. The largest resort hotels on both islands have activities that continue around the clock.

Gambling

The casinos at the Marriott Resort on Cable Beach (Tel. 327-6200), Atlantis on Paradise Island (Tel. 363-3000), and the Princess Resort on Grand Bahama (Tel. 352-7811) all offer roulette, craps, and blackjack as well as slot machines. The slot machines operated 24 hours a day, but there are limited hours for the gaming tables: at Atlantis they're open 10am–4am, at Princess Casino and the Marriott 9am–3am.

Floor Shows

If gambling is not your cup of tea, allow yourself to be dazzled by one of the nightly Las Vegas–style floor shows at the Mar-

Junkanoo

A uniquely Bahamian celebration, Junkanoo has been compared to the Carnival in Rio or Mardi Gras in New Orleans. Starting in the early hours of 26 December, Junkanoo is a Bahamian-style celebration that's guaranteed to keep you awake. Central to the festivities is a street parade with rhythmical musical accompaniment made up of a number of teams who work all year to create fantastic, colorful, and elaborate costumes. Dancers course through the streets along the street showing off their artwork accompanied by other merrymakers playing an assortment of instruments. Bugles, whistles, cowbells, maracas, and homemade goatskin drums make for an upbeat sound all of its own. On the "official" nights of Junkanoo—26 December and 31 December—the crowds are huge, as all the islanders get involved.

The origins of the word Junkanoo are obscure. Some say that it is derived from John Canoe, a legendary African chief, others that it comes from the French *gens inconnus*, meaning unknown people, because of the masks worn during the parade.

riott, Atlantis, or the Princess. For information about the Princess cabaret, call 352-6721; for the Marriott Palace Revue, call 327-6200, for the Atlantis, call 363-3000.

CHILDREN

There's nothing young visitors to the Bahamas like better than a sandy beach and the sea. Most big resorts have clean, safe beaches where children can frolic and play.

Older children enjoy snorkeling or taking a ride on a glass-bottom boat. Back on land, some children enjoy having their hair braided.

Other attractions for younger visitors include:

Horse-drawn surrey rides. A great way to see all the sights of Nassau; the horses are trained and the pace is slow.

Bahama boogie! Caribe show dancers give off some island-style heat.

Pirates of Nassau Attraction. Discover the pirate lifestyle.

The Dig, Atlantis Paradise Beach. Explore the world of the fictitious "Atlanteans" and watch the sharks and other sea creatures in the biggest aquarium in the world.

Crystal Cay. Explore beneath the sea, without getting wet.

Dolphin Encounters. Blue Lagoon, New Providence, or UNEXSO on Grand Bahama. Swim with the dolphins.

EATING OUT

Finding something appealing for dinner is not going to be a problem in the Bahamas. The expansion of international cuisine over the last decade, combined with nutritious and tasty local dishes, means that there should always be something on the menu that will please. In the main islands you'll have a choice of everything from fine restaurants with extensive wine lists, to harborside burger bars, to small roadside stalls, where the locals grab lunch or a snack on the way home from work. Things in the Out Islands are generally more relaxed, with fewer opportunities for formal dining, though each major harbor has its share of lively bars and restaurants.

On the Out Islands you'll find that many restaurants stop serving dinner as early as 9pm, and they may close earlier if they have no customers. It always helps to call ahead, especially if you travel out of season. On the main islands, which have a higher population and more visitors, restaurants are open for longer hours and there is more choice and variety of dining styles. It is important to make a reservation at the most popular spots to guarantee your table.

What to Eat

Conch

The Bahamas is blessed with fertile seas and it enjoys the bounty of the ocean—an abundance of fresh fish that comes in daily—but its "pièce de resistance" has to be the conch (pronounced "konk"), a shellfish that everyone will tell you is the Bahamian aphrodisiac. It is impossible to overestimate the value of this food to the national diet. Almost all Bahamians eat it regularly. A mollusk that inhabits a rather fine shell, conch is almost 100 percent protein. The creatures are gath-

Whether "cracked" with peas and rice (above) or raw in a salad, delicious fresh conch is always on the menu.

ered from the sea-bed and taken from their shells, and the flesh is then tenderized and prepared in an amazing variety of methods. (Most shells are discarded, but you'll find the more attractive ones for sale as souvenirs throughout the islands.)

The Bahamians' favorite way to eat conch is in salad. The raw flesh is finely sliced and mixed with onions, peppers, and tomatoes, then covered with lemon and sour orange juice. The result is a fresh-tasting, nutritious mixture. "Cracked conch" is made by dipping the sliced flesh in a fine cracker-crumb batter and frying it, and conch "burgers" are fashioned out of ground conch mixed with onion and cereal—these patties rival the best beef burgers. Hearty conch chowder is a staple on menus throughout the islands—the native Bahamian version has a slightly spicy tomato and onion base, but you'll also find creamy New England–style on many menus. Both are extremely delicious and filling; order the small portion if you want to be able to eat the rest of your meal.

Bounty of the Sea

You can be guaranteed that the seafood you are served in the Bahamas will always be fresh, as small boats come in daily with catches of the most amazing array of sea creatures. A restaurant's "catch of the day" is often the tastiest and freshest option. Grouper is one of the most common choices, but, depending on the season, it could also be tuna, snapper, wahoo, or kingfish; whatever the species, however, the simply served fillets, goujons (finger-shaped pieces), or whole fish are always superb. Lobster is always tasty, though Maine lobster may be frozen.

Living the good life! Patrons at the Blue Bar café, Pink Sands, Harbour Island.

Crawfish and crab also appear on menus in season. Crawfish, with their characteristic fleshy tail, must now be left alone to breed between April and August, so if you find it on a menu during that period it will be frozen. Crabs are abundant on certain islands in May, June, and July. Traditionally they were a feast of plenty but with the advent of freezers crabs are enjoyed by locals throughout the year. They are also harvested by the local people and shipped to New Providence where they are highly sought after and fetch a high price.

Side Dishes

Most main dishes are accompanied by a dish of rice and peas. This popular side-dish originated as a cheap and nutritious option in colonial times; it was often served as a meal in itself when money was scarce. The "peas" in question are actually red or kidney beans. The rice is cooked slowly together with tomato paste, onions, thyme, black pepper, and other seasonings; sometimes a little drop of coconut milk is added for a creamier consistency. If you don't like rice, you can always opt for French fries, offered as an alternative on most menus.

Other traditional Bahamian staples include Johnny cake (a heavy cassava bread) and sweet potato bread. Even the standard varieties of bread in the Bahamas are slightly sweet.

Desserts

The Bahamas has a number of native citrus fruits that are used to great effect in marinades for fish and other seafood. Other native fruits available seasonally include mangoes, sapodillas, and sugar apples. Very small and very sweet pineapples are grown on Eleuthera and coconuts are abundant throughout the islands; both of these ingredients make their way into delicious sweet pies and pastries. Most of the islands have at least one local bakery that's open every day except Sunday.

Nothing is more Bahamian than guava duff, uncompromisingly fattening but difficult to resist. A cake-like pie served with rum sauce, it's one of the best dishes to come from island kitchens.

International Cuisine

You'll find versions of all Bahamian dishes on the menus of the large hotels; the resorts on the main islands and many larger settlements on the Out Islands, however, also offer a full range of international cuisine. In most spots you'll have no problem ordering a steak or a bottle of fine wine. Food is shipped the short distance from Florida every day and is extremely fresh.

Both European and American cuisine can be found in many restaurants. Asian influences are beginning to make inroads. You'll find the greatest choice on New Providence and Grand Bahama. Many hotels have more than one restaurant—Sandals on Cable Beach has five and the Atlantis Paradise Island has 20, so it will be hard for even the most daring palates to get bored. Head out from the hotel into Nassau or Freeport/Lucaya and there's plenty of choice in all price brackets.

If you have a hankering for fast food you can pick from one of the many burger bars and pizza places. Some pizza companies will deliver—if you can't bear heading out to a restaurant.

What to Drink

In the Bahamas the legal age for drinking alcohol is 18.

Beer

The Bahamas produces its own beer called Kalik (pronounced "k'lik"), said to be named after the rhythmic sound of the bands playing at Junckanoo as they k-lick-k-lick their way along the streets. The beer is light and clean tasting, perfect to drown the thirst on a hot day. It must be served cold. A range of American and European beers can be found at a higher price.

Rum

Bacardi is the rum of the Bahamas, particularly since Castro came to power in Cuba and production moved away from there. No matter which rum cocktails or punches you chose, watch out, because they all "pack a punch." Many bars have their own special recipes, but most will combine rum with fresh fruit juice, lime, or coconut milk. The Goombay Smash (generally made with rum, coconut rum, and pineapple juice) is known across the Bahamas, as is the Bahama Mama (rum, crème de cassis, grenadine, lemon juice and a dusting of nutmeg), though the piña colada (rum, coconut cream, and pineapple juice frothed with crushed ice) remains a favorite. Frozen daiquiris (rum, fruit juice, cream, and crushed ice blended to the consistency of a thick milk shake) are offered everywhere, and another favorite —also said by Bahamians to be an aphrodisiac—is gin and fresh coconut juice.

The Bahamas played an important part in the production of a famous European drink: Cascarilla, the bark of the Croton eleuteria tree, found almost exclusively on

Cocktail heaven: indulge in a Bahama Mama, or a Goombay Smash, or...

Crooked and Aklins Islands, is dried and shipped to Italy for use as an ingredient in the secret recipe for the drink Campari.

Nonalcoholic Drinks

The choice of fruit juices is almost infinite. You'll find single juices or blends in every bar or restaurant. All the leading international brands of soda are also readily available. On the Out Islands you may also find "lemonade," usually freshly made and delicious, with a real hint of the actual fruit—very refreshing on a hot day.

INDEX

Acklins Island 76-77, 96

Albert Lowe Museum 58

Alice Town 70

Andros 11, 13, 21, 63-65, 71, 85-86, 91-93, 96-97

Aquarium (Paradise Island) 38

Arawak Cay 42

Ardastra Gardens, Zoo, and Conservation Centre 41

Art Deco District (Miami) 80

Atlantis Paradise Island 25, 29, 37, 100, 106

Balcony House 29, 32

Ben's Cave 49-50

Berry Islands 71

Bimini 22, 37, 69-70, 88, 92, 95-96

Blackbeard's Tower 43

Blue Lagoon and the Dolphin Experience 39

Cable Beach 42-43, 91, 99, 106

Cat Island 7, 19, 51, 71, 76, 96

Chub Cay 71

Clarence Town 76

Cockburn Town 74

Coconut Grove (Miami) 79

Coral Gables (Miami) 78

Crooked Island 76-77

Crystal Cay 29, 42, 101

Deadman's Cay 76

Disney Cruises 83

Dixon Hill Lighthouse 75

Dunmore Town 59

Elbow Cay 55, 57

Eleuthera 12, 14-18, 26, 51, 58-63, 88, 90-91, 96, 105

Exuma Cays Land & Sea Park 69

Family Islands 10, 25, 52

Fort Charlotte 23, 29, 41

Fort Fincastle 29, 32-33

Fort Montague 43

Freeport-Lucaya 44-45, 48-49, 51, 54

George Town 51, 67, 85, 88, 97

Glass Window 61-62

Gold Rock Beach 50-51

Goombay Market 46

Government House 29, 35

Governor's Harbour 59, 62

Grand Bahama Island 10, 43, 53, 91

Graycliff Mansion 33, 35

Great Abaco 20, 51, 53-54

Great Guana Cay 51, 56

Green Turtle Cay 56, 58, 90, 96

Gregory Town 16, 62, 88, 90

Harbour Island 12, 17-18, 35, 51, 59-62, 92, 104

Hope Town 54-55, 89-90

Inagua National Park 77

John F. Kennedy Space Center 80-81

Landfall Park 75
Little Abaco 53
Little Havana (Miami) 78
Long Island 74-76, 88, 93
Lucaya National Park 44, 49
Lucayan Golf & Country Club 48

Man-O-War Cay 55-56
Marsh Harbour 20, 54-56, 90, 98
Mayaguana Island 77
Mount Alvernia 7, 72

Nassau 8, 10, 12, 16-19, 21-35, 39-43, 49, 52, 54, 67, 69-71, 76, 83, 85-89, 91, 94, 98-99, 101, 106
New Plymouth 57-58

Ocean Den 77
Orlando 81, 83-84

Paradise Island 21, 25, 29, 32, 35-40, 43, 91, 99-100, 106
Parrot Jungle's Garden of the Groves 48
Petersons Cay 49, 51
Pirates of Nassau 29, 33-34, 101
Pompey Museum of Slavery and Emancipation 33
Port Canaveral 81, 83
Port Lucaya 11, 44-47, 86-87
Potter's Cay 40
Preacher's Cave 61
Prince George Wharf 27, 31
Princess Casino 46, 100

Public Buildings of Parliament Square 31

Rand Memorial Nature Centre 44, 48
Rawson Square 31
Red Bays 63
Rock Sound 63

San Salvador 14-15, 26, 71-75, 88, 93, 96
Sanctuary Bay 47
Sea World of Florida 84
Seaquarium (Miami) 80
South Beach (Miami) 80
Spanish Wells 14, 59-60
Stanial Cay 69
Stella Maris 74-76, 93-94
Stocking Cay 66-67
Straw Market 28, 30, 59, 67

The Cloisters 29, 38-39
The Ferry 40, 55-56, 67-68
Three Sisters Rock 68
Tongue of the Ocean 11, 64, 71, 92, 96
Treasure Cay 51, 56
Turtle Cove 76

UNEXSO Dolphin Experience 44, 47
Universal Studios Florida 84

Walt Disney World 81-84
Water Tower 29, 32
West End 22, 49, 52
Wyannie Malone Historical Museum 55

HANDY TRAVEL TIPS

An A–Z Summary of Practical Information

A Accommodations 111
Airports 112

B Bicycle Rental 112
Budgeting for Your
Trip 113

C Camping 113
Car Rental 114
Climate 115
Clothing 115
Complaints 116
Crime and Safety 116
Customs and Entry
Requirements 116

D Driving 117

E Electricity 118
Embassies, Consulates,
and High
Commissions 118
Emergencies 118

G Gay and Lesbian
Travelers 119
Getting to the
Bahamas 119
Guides and Tours 120

H Health and Medical
Care 120

Hithhiking 121

L Language 121
Laundry and Dry
Cleaning 122

M Maps 122
Media 122
Money Matters 123

O Opening Hours 123

P Police 123
Post Offices 124
Public Holidays 124
Public Transportation
124

R Religion 126

T Telephone 126
Tickets 126
Time Zones 127
Tipping 127
Toilets 127
Tourist Information
127

W Weights and
Measures 129

W Youth Hostels 129

A

ACCOMMODATIONS (See CAMPING and YOUTH HOSTELS)

The Bahamas has a full range of accommodations, from beach cottages to luxury all-inclusive hotels, but it specializes in high-end "get-away-from-it-all" paradise resorts. You'll encounter several different kinds of room-and-meal-plan packages: AI (All-Inclusive) means that all resort services and activities, sports facilities, meals, and drinks are included in the price. AP (American Plan) provides breakfast, lunch, and dinner along with lodging, whereas MAP (Modified American Plan) provides only breakfast and dinner. EP (European Plan) rates are for the room alone, without meals.

The Bahamas Ministry of Tourism's *Where Shall We Stay?* hotel guide lists comprehensive information about all hotels throughout the islands. As a general rule, the larger resorts are found on New Providence and Grand Bahama. All together, the Out Islands have only around 1,500 hotel rooms total; many of these offer a luxury getaway experience, or they focus on specific activities, such as diving or bone fishing. Many large resorts offer extensive sporting facilities, such as golf courses, equestrian centers, or scuba diving schools. Wedding packages and honeymoon "specials" are also available, with quite a range in quality and price. Although All-Inclusive hotels offer all facilities for one price, it is important to do some checking on the facilities beforehand, as these do vary. Some All-inclusive establishments still assess extra charges for certain activities or for special "luxury" foods or premium brands of alcohol.

A number of the Out Islands also offer a range of private villas for rent. Hope Town on Elbow Cay, in particular, has comprehensive listings of well-maintained properties; contact Hope Town Hideaways (Tel. 366-0224; fax 336-0434). If you want a room that floats you can rent a boat and either live at the marina or sail around from one cay to another; try The Moorings, which has a variety of sailboats for rent, with or without a crew (Tel. 367-4000; fax 367-4004; website <www.moorings.com>).

Bahamas

AIRPORTS

A number of the Bahamian Islands have airports with immigration and customs facilities that can serve as ports of entry. Most visitors enter through **Nassau International Airport** on New Providence, which is also the main hub for Bahamasair flights to the other islands. Direct service from the US is also available to the international airports in Freeport (Grand Bahama), Bimini, San Salvador, Eleuthera, Abaco, and Andros.

American Airlines, American Eagle, and Bahamasair offer direct flights to Nassau from Miami and a number of other cities in the US and Canada. British Airways runs direct flights from London several times a week (with connecting flights from other British and European airports). Citizens of Australia or New Zealand can travel either via London or Los Angeles.

There are also a number of smaller airports throughout the Bahamas that are used primarily by private planes and small charters: Marsh Harbour, Treasure Cay, and Walkers Cay on Abaco; Andros Town, Congo Town, and San Andros on Andros; Chub Cay and Great Harbour Cay on the Berry Islands; South Bimini; New Bight on Cat Island; Governors Harbour, North Eleuthera, and Rock Sound on Eleuthera; George Town and Moss Town on Great Exuma Island; Matthew Town on Great Inagua; Cockburn Town on San Salvador; and Stella Maris on Long Island.

BICYCLE RENTAL

Many of the Out Islands and cays are flat and compact and have little traffic, which makes them ideal for exploring by bicycle. The daily rate for bikes varies from $10 to $15, a little less if you take one for a longer period of time. Some hotels and cottages supply a bicycle for your use (it's usually included in the price of your stay). The Honda Cycle Shop on Queen's Highway on Grand Bahama (Tel. 352-7035) and the Bike Shop in Hope Town, Elbow Cay (Tel. 336-0292) have bikes for rent.

BUDGETING for YOUR TRIP

The following list will give you some idea of prices for services and activities in the Bahamas:

Bicycle rental. $20 a day on New Providence and Grand Bahama; $10–$15 a day on the Out Islands.

Car rental. $70–$90 a day for a mid-range, medium-sized car.

Drinks. Glass of beer, $2.50, glass of wine, $3.50, cocktail, $5, cup of coffee, $1.25.

Golf-cart rental. $35–$45, for transportation on the Out Islands.

Hotels. Double room at a moderately priced hotel, $130 per night. (See RECOMMENDED HOTELS on page 130.)

Jitneys. From Nassau Town to Cable Beach, 75¢; from Freeport to Lucaya, $1.

Meals. Lunch at a moderately priced establishment, $12 per person (without drinks); dinner at a moderately priced establishment, $25 per person (without drinks). (See RECOMMENDED RESTAURANTS on page 139.)

Sport-fishing boat. $300 for ½ day, $400 for full day.

Taxis. From Nassau International Airport to Cable Beach, $12; from Nassau International Airport to Paradise Island, $25; from Treasure Cay Airport to ferry dock, $3 per person.

Water taxis. From Abaco to Green Turtle Cay, $8 one-way; from Eleuthera to Harbour Island, $3 one-way.

CAMPING

Camping is not illegal on the Bahamas, but it is not recommended. There are no official camp sites.

Bahamas

CAR RENTAL

Many of the islands are small and unsuitable for cars. Only a few of the Out Islands—Eleuthera and Great Abaco Island, for example—are really big enough to warrant getting a car for exploring. Having a car on New Providence and Grand Bahama, however, does give you extra flexibility, especially if you want to break away from fixed tour itineraries.

All the major car-rental companies operate on New Providence and Grand Bahama; you can pick your car up at the airport or have it delivered to your hotel. Rentals cost between $60 and $90 a day, depending on the size of the car and the season (prices are higher in winter). In high season, make a reservation well in advance, because demand is high. The international companies are more expensive than the local companies, but their cars are newer and better maintained. Be aware that many rental agencies offer "new" cars, which are in fact two or three years old. Always satisfy yourself as to the age and condition of the car before confirming the reservation, and remember to specify whether you want a manual or automatic transmission.

All national driving licenses are recognized by the rental companies; drivers must have held a license for at least one year. In the US, some insurance companies cover rental cars; check to see whether you are covered on your policy or through your credit card before purchasing insurance. Damage waiver is recommended—this will add around $15 per day to the cost.

Avis. New Providence; Tel. 377-7121. Grand Bahama; Tel. 352-7666.

Budget. Nassau International Airport; tel. 377-9000. Paradise Island Airport; Tel. 363-3095.

Dollar. New Providence; Tel. 377-8308. Grand Bahama; Tel. 352-9325.

On the smaller cays, golf carts and scooters are popular means of transport. Both are fun to drive and provide a great alternative for travelers on a budget. Scooters in particular make for more adventurous exploring, giving you easy access to smaller roads and byways. Drivers need a valid license and insurance. Helmets are mandatory and are usually included in the rental price. The average rate is $50 a day. In Nassau try Bowes Scooter Rental at Prince George's Wharf; on Grand Bahama, check with the Honda Cycle Shop on Queen's Highway (Tel. 352-7035). On Green Turtle Cay, contact C and D Rental (Tel. 365-4084); on Elbow Cay, Hope Town Cart Rentals (Tel. 336-0064); on Harbour Island, Island Treasures (Tel. 365-6072).

CLIMATE

The Bahamas has a semitropical climate, cooled in summer by the trade winds and warmed in the winter by the Gulf Stream currents. Temperatures range between 70 and 80 degrees fahrenheit; it rarely falls below 60, nor does it often rise over 90. Winter (Nov–Apr) tends to be cooler and dryer, summer (May–Oct) warmer and wetter; rain showers can occur at all times of the year. Sea temperatures range from 75°F (24°C) in winter and 83°F (28°C) in summer. Hurricane season falls between June and November; approaching storms (both in and out of hurricane season) are usually forecast well in advance.

The following chart gives the average monthly temperatures and rainfall for the area:

	J	F	M	A	M	J	J	A	S	O	N	D
Temperature °C	21	21	22	24	25	27	27	28	27	26	23	22
Temperature °F	70	70	72	75	75	78	78	79	78	77	74	72
Rainfall inches	1.9	1.6	1.4	1.9	4.8	9.2	6.1	6.3	7.7	8.3	2.3	1.5

CLOTHING

Lightweight clothing is appropriate throughout the year—many people manage happily with T-shirts and shorts during the day with something a little more formal in the evening, perhaps a sports jacket for men and smart casual for women. Cotton or breathable blends are ideal. In winter, it pays to have a light sweater along for the occasional cool evening. If you intend to visit any of the Out Island towns, more conservative clothing may be appropriate. Beachwear is acceptable only in the immediate area of the beach on all Bahamian islands.

Bahamas

A hat and sunglasses are important, as the sun is very strong, especially in the middle of the day. When you first arrive, always make sure that you wear something like a lightweight long-sleeved shirt to prevent getting a sunburn. Footwear should be light and comfortable, a pair of sandals or flip-flops for the beach, along with a smarter choice for evenings. If you plan to walk any distance, even around town, a comfortable pair of walking shoes or sneakers is indispensable.

COMPLAINTS

Complaints should be taken up in the first instance with the person or organization concerned. If the situation is not resolved, contact the Visitor Relations Unit of the Bahamas Ministry of Tourism, Bay Street, Nassau; Tel. 322-7500.

CRIME and SAFETY

In Nassau and Freeport, crime has become a matter of concern to police and tourism authorities. Petty theft and break-in robbery is a problem; some of it is drug-related. Common-sense precautions include: locking valuables in your hotel's safe deposit boxes; not leaving anything important in your rental car, even if it's locked; not leaving belongings unattended on the beach if you go for a swim or snorkel; not wearing expensive jewelry or watches in public; and not walking after dark on side streets.

The situation is quite different on the Out Islands, where honesty is so taken for granted that many people still don't bother to lock their doors. This does not mean, however, that you should abandon common sense.

CUSTOMS and ENTRY REQUIREMENTS

Visitors from the US do not need a passport to enter the Bahamas; a birth certificate or driver's license is sufficient. British and Commonwealth citizens must present a full passport and evidence of onward or return transportation for stays not exceeding 30 days.

Citizens of Ireland and South Africa need a full passport and evidence of onward or return transportation for stays not exceeding 3 months.

The Bahamas has a departure tax of $15 from New Providence and the Out Islands, $20 from Grand Bahama.

The following items may be brought into the Bahamas without paying duty: 200 cigarettes or 50 cigars, .45 kg (1 pound) of tobacco, 1.14 *l* (1 quart) of spirits, and 1.14 *l* (1 quart) of wine.

D

DRIVING

Probably the Commonwealth's most noticeable reminder of the British era is driving on the left. Vehicles in the Bahamas, however, come with the steering wheel either on the right or on the left. Both New Providence and Grand Bahama have good main roads. Many roadways and streets in New Providence are narrow (and busy); they tend to be wider on Grand Bahama. On the Out Islands the roads have very little traffic; most of the major roads are in good shape, but some of the smaller ones are unsurfaced and full of potholes.

Speed limits are 25 mph (40 km/h) in built-up areas, 40 mph (65 km/h) outside the towns. Be aware that local drivers may not adhere to these limits. Always drive with care and attention. Roundabouts (traffic circles) are numerous on New Providence and Grand Bahama; yield to the right to the traffic that is already in the circle. It's against the law to drive or ride on a motorcycle without a helmet.

Fuel is easy to find on New Providence and Grand Bahama but not so plentiful on the Out Islands, so always make adequate provisions before setting out. Service stations are open Monday through Saturday and they take credit cards. In the event of a breakdown there are no emergency services as such. Always make sure that you have the name and telephone number of a reliable mechanic just in case; your rental company should supply one to you. On the Out Islands it's also advisable to leave your travel plans with your hotel reception so that if there is a problem they have a schedule which they can follow.

Bahamas

Fluid measures

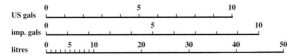

Distance

E

ELECTRICITY

The Bahamas has standard North American current, 120 volts, 60 cycles AC. Visitors from North America do not need adapters for their electrical appliances.

EMBASSIES, CONSULATES, HIGH COMMISSIONS

Only a few countries maintain formal diplomatic posts in Nassau:

Canada: Canadian Honorary Consul, P.O. Box SS-6371, Nassau; Tel. 393-2123/4.

UK: The British High Commission, BITCO Building (3rd Floor), East Street, P.O. Box N-7516, Nassau; Tel. 325-7471.

US: Embassy of the United States of America, Mosmar Building, Queen Street, P.O. Box N-8197, Nassau; Tel. 322-1181.

EMERGENCIES

For police and ambulance, dial **911**, for fire, dial **411**.
The Bahamas Ministry of Tourism on New Providence has an emergency number; Tel. 326-HELP (4357). On Grand Bahama; Tel. 352-8044/5.

G

GAY and LESBIAN TRAVELERS

The Bahamas remains a fairly conservative place and gay men and lesbians have very little public presence. Strict laws against homosexual activity are still in effect, and penalties can be severe.

GETTING to the BAHAMAS

By air. Nassau International Airport is the major gateway and serves as the hub for travel to the Out Islands. Miami, just 40 minutes flying time from Nassau, is one of the major points of departure from mainland US. Bahamasair (Tel. 800-222-2462) and American Airlines/American Eagle (Tel. 800-433-7300) both have direct flights from Miami. Delta Airlines has daily direct flights from New York and Atlanta. Air Canada (Tel. 800-268-7240) flies direct from Montreal and Toronto. British Airways (UK Tel. 0345/222-111) has non-stop service from London-Gatwick as well as a number of flights through Miami. Comair flies from Fort Lauderdale, Florida, to Nassau and Freeport.

British and European travelers can fly via London or the US (Miami or New York). Australians and New Zealanders can pick up a connection to the Bahamas through the US (Los Angeles to Miami) or the UK; both directions involve long journeys and possibly a stopover or two.

Many other scheduled airlines and charter companies offer services from the US and Europe, depending on the time of year, with more services flying during high season. Package holidays are also available. Consult a travel agent for the most appropriate service for your plans.

Cruises. Nassau is included on many Caribbean cruise itineraries, even on some of the shorter (3–4-day) packages. There is an almost bewildering number of choices: All cruise companies offer several different packages that vary in quality and price, and, in some cases, the type of passenger they cater to. Some are designed for more mature travelers, some for the young and lively, some for gay travelers, some for families. It is important to research these choices carefully before making a firm booking.

Several of the leading cruise companies are based in Miami: **Carnival Cruise Lines** (Tel. 800-438-6744 or 305/599-2600) is good for the young, party-hardy crowd; **Royal Caribbean** (Tel. 800-327-6700) caters to many different tastes with mass-market cruises on massive ships; and **Holland America Line** (Tel. 800-426-0327, or 206/281-3535) has a number of options for more mature travelers. Several companies offer shorter trips with fewer frills. For example, **Majesty Cruise Lines** (Tel. 800-532-7788) specializes in cruises just off the coast of Florida; one of their boats, the *Royal Majesty,* is non-smoking.

Port Canaveral, east of Orlando and the Disney parks, is another point of departure for cruises to the Bahamas. The *Disney Wonder* (Tel. 407/566-7000) departs from Canaveral's North Port and stops at Nassau before moving on to Disney's private Bahamian Cay. **Premier Cruise Lines** (Tel. 800-473-3262) offers short family-style trips.

Departure tax is $15 from New Providence (Nassau) and $20 from Grand Bahama.

GUIDES and TOURS

A number of companies offer tours of New Providence and Nassau Town. **Reliable Tours** escorts small groups in buses (12–15 passengers) or limousine tours (27 Clifton St., P.O. Box CB-13036, Nassau; Tel. 328-6500; fax 328-3906; e-mail <badwolf@bahamas.net.bs>). On Grand Bahama, contact **H. Forbes Charter Company,** which runs several different tours, including a comprehensive ½-day tour of the Freeport-Lucaya area (Tel. 352-9311: they have an office in the Bahama Princess Country Club).

H

HEALTH and MEDICAL CARE

The standards of hygiene are generally high in the Bahamas. The tap water is drinkable, though bottled water is found in all supermarkets and grocery stores. There are some minor nuisances: Mosquitoes can be a problem, especially just after sunset, so cover up or apply insect repellent. Sand flies, called "no see 'ums" by locals because they are so small, can bite, so carry repellent with you at all times just in case run into them. Be careful not to step on the spiny sea urchins while snorkeling or diving; the spines will embed themselves into your flesh and can become infected. Go easy on the alcohol, especially in the sunshine, as this could lead to dehydration. And take time to build up your tan, starting with only brief sessions on the beach, to avoid sunburn and sunstroke.

Pharmacies on New Providence and Grand Bahama Island are well stocked. Of you're traveling to the Out Islands, however, it would be sensible to anticipate your needs and take what you need with you. The large hotels have a doctor on call to take care of any medical problems that might come up; contact the front desk to arrange a visit. Since you will have to pay for any medical treatment you need while in the Bahamas, it is important that you take out adequate health insurance before you depart. Any pre-existing condition should always be taken into account. A serious accident or medical probelem may necessitate repatriation or transfer to a hospital in the US, which is extremely expensive.

The two main hospitals are the Princess Margaret (Sands Lane, Nassau; Tel. 322-2861) and the Rand Memorial Hospital (East Atlantic Drive, Freeport; Tel. 352-6735).

HITCHHIKING

Hitchhiking is illegal in the Bahamas, although on the Out Islands, where cars are few, it's not at all unusual for neighbors to offer other neighbors, and the occasional tourist, a lift.

LANGUAGE

The national language of the Bahamas is English, though residents speak a mixture of British English, American English, and African Creole that outsiders sometimes find difficult to understand. And what's more, different islands have their own linguistic peculiarities. You'll no doubt have to ask for a translation now and then, which Bahamians will cheerfully try to provide.

LAUNDRY and DRY CLEANING

All the major hotels provide laundry and dry cleaning services and many also supply iron and ironing board as standard amenities in the rooms. On the Out Islands, however, service may not be so comprehensive and dry cleaning is practically unknown.

M

MAPS

Many of the main resorts provide free maps that will guide you to the main tourist attractions in the surrounding territory. They are not particularly detailed and are not topographical, but on many islands they are adequate for sightseeing. If you intend to navigate between islands, detailed marine charts or aerial charts are available from ships supplies stores and general aviation units.

MEDIA

The Bahamas has only one TV channel, ZNS, which is beamed from Nassau to Grand Bahama, Eleuthera, Abaco, Andros, and most of the other northern islands. Satellite and cable networks from the US now reach the major islands and many Florida stations can be picked up throughout the Bahamas with varying degrees of clarity. Many hotels and some bars have CNN and ESPN, a small number even have the BBC News Channel broadcast from London.

ZNS also operates three radio stations and a number of stations from Florida can be picked up on New Providence, Grand Bahama, and Andros.

The major Bahamian newspapers are the *Nassau Guardian* (morning) and the *Tribune* (afternoon), both sold at news agents and kiosks. US and major British newspapers can be found at large resort hotels and cruise ports (the British newspapers will be one or two days old).

MONEY MATTERS

The national currency of the Bahamas is the Bahamian dollar, which is the divided into 100 cents. The currency is issued in coins of 1¢, 5¢, 10¢, 25¢, and 50¢ and notes of $1, $5, $10, $20, $50, and $100. The Bahamian dollar is linked to, and trades on a par with the US dollar, and it would be wise to trade any Bahamian Dollars for US Dollars before you leave the islands. US dollars are accepted as freely as Bahamian dollars in shops and restaurants. Other foreign nationals would find it easier to bring cash in US dollars rather than their own currency. Travelers checks are widely accepted; checks in US$ are the most practical. Credit cards are widely accepted on the main islands.

International ATMs, which accept credit cards and international bank cards, can be found only on New Providence and Grand Bahama. They are located at Royal Bank of Scotland branches at the Tourist Information Centre in Rawson Square Nassau, Nassau International Airport, the Marriott Casino on Cable Beach, and the Atlantis Casino, Paradise Island. The Bank of Nova Scotia on Bay Street, Nassau also has an international ATM. On Grand Bahama you'll find them at the Bahamas Princess casino. There are Royal Bank of Canada machines at East Mall/Explorers Way and at the Boulevard service station on Sunrise Highway.

OPENING HOURS

Banks are open Monday–Thursday 9:30am–3pm and Friday 9:30am–5pm. Most shops are open 9am–5pm, but in tourist areas and in high season, opening times are extended into the evening.

POLICE

The friendly and helpful Bahamian police, sporting black trousers or skirts with red stripes and white short-sleeved shirts, patrol the streets of Nassau town on foot; on the rest of New Providence and on Grand Bahama they travel in police cruisers. Call **911** for emergencies.

POST OFFICES

It costs 40¢ to send a postcard from the Bahamas to any destination. Rates for letters (half ounce) are: 55¢ to North America, 60¢ to Europe, and 70¢ to Australasia. Post offices are open Monday–Friday 8:30–5:30, Saturday 8:30–12:30. Nassau's main post office is on Shirley Street, Freeport's is on Explorer's Way. Most hotels in the islands provide postage service for guests. The postal service from the Bahamas is slow, however; so if you have anything urgent or valuable to send, it may be better to use a commercial mail service.

PUBLIC HOLIDAYS

January 1	*New Years Day*
March/April	*Good Friday, Easter Monday*
May/June	*Whit Monday (7 weeks after Easter)*
1st Friday in June	*Labour Day*
June 10	*Independence Day*
1st Monday in August	*Emancipation Day*
October 12	*Discovery Day*
December 25	*Christmas*
December 26	*Boxing Day*

PUBLIC TRANSPORTATION

Between the Islands

Bahamasair (Tel. 377-5505 or 800-222-4262) offers service to each of the main islands from Nassau International Airport, the airline's hub. There are daily flights to Grand Bahama; Marsh Harbour and Treasure Cay on Abaco; North Eleuthera, Governor's Harbour, and Rock Sound on Eleuthera Island; Georgetown on Exuma; San Salvador; and Andros Town, San Andros, and South Andros on Andros. To travel from one island to another you will always have to travel via Nassau. Always allow at least a couple of hours for transfers as flights are often late.

A number of private charter airlines operate between Nassau and some of the islands. Some private charter companies will create a customized itinerary for you or fly you to a particular island, but this can be expensive, especially for a single traveler since you pay for the plane journey rather than just for one seat.

You can also use the Bahamian mail boat service to travel to any of the inhabited islands. This is the cheapest way to get around ($25–$80 round-trip, depending on the route). It's also one of the best ways to get to know Bahamians. Trips can last between 3 and 18 hours one-way, and cabins are available on some of the longer journeys. Contact the harbormaster for schedules and fares: on Potters Cay in Nassau; Tel. 393-1064.

On the Islands

New Providence. A jitney (small bus) service covers the entire island (fare: 75¢ per trip). The hub of the local bus system is Nassau. Buses run from Bay Street to the eastern and western ends of the island (maximum fare: $1.50); there is no bus service from the airport terminals or to Paradise Island. Taxis post the fares to the most popular destinations. Nassau town can be toured by horse-drawn "surrey" for $5 per person. The surreys wait in front of the cruise-port dock and are available every day, though they do not operate between 2 and 4pm in the summer, to protect the horses from the intense heat.

Grand Bahama Island. Limited jitney service operates from the Pub on the Mall at International Bazaar to Port Lucaya ($1 each way).

The Out Islands. There is little or no public transport on the Out Islands. Taxis are available for transfers or sightseeing tours; depending on the size of the island or cay, you can rent either a car, bicycle, or golf cart to explore on your own.

R

RELIGION

Religion is alive and well in the Bahamas. The predominant faith is Christianity and many denominations are represented, including Anglican, Baptist, Christian Science, Church of God, Hebrew Congregation, Jehovah's Witnesses, Lutheran, Methodist, Plymouth Brethren, Presbyterian, Roman Catholic, and Seventh Day Adventist.

T

TELEPHONE

The Bahamas has a direct-dial digital system, but the service in the Out Islands can be temperamental. Many large hotels have direct-dial phones in each room; some of the smaller hotels only have a phone at the hotel reception. The cost of making calls from hotels is always high. There are also public telephones throughout Nassau and Grand Bahama and in the main towns of the Out Islands. Phone cards can be used in certain public phones; look for a sign on the phone stating which cards work—AT&T, USA Direct, etc. BaTelCo, the Bahamas telephone company, is gradually replacing old equipment, but you may still run across old-style coin-operated phones, which take 25¢ coins. New telephones take BaTelCo telephone cards, which are available in denominations of $5, $10, $20, and $50; you can buy them from BaTelCo offices—the most accessible is on East Bay Street in Nassau—or from the reception desk at some hotels.

800 numbers in the US can be accessed from the Bahamas by dialing 1-800 followed by the last seven digits of the number; these are charged at the rate of 99¢ per minute.

Emergency numbers are **919** for police and ambulance, **411** for fire.

TICKETS

Tickets for the floor shows at the Grand Bahama Princess Resort, Atlantis Paradise Island, and the Marriott Cable Beach can be bought from the box offices at each of those hotels.

TIME ZONES

The Bahamas operates on Eastern Standard Time, which is 5 hours behind Greenwich Mean Time. Eastern Daylight Saving Time is adopted in the summer on the same schedule used in North America. See table below:

Los Angeles	Chicago	New York	**Bahamas**	London	Sydney
9am	11am	noon	**noon**	5pm	3am

TIPPING

Tipping is standard for restaurant and bar service in the Bahamas; 15% is the usual amount. Many establishments automatically add a service charge to the bill—this policy should be printed on the menu or the bill if it is in effect. In general, porters are tipped $1 per bag, chambermaids $2 a day, and taxi drivers and tour guides 15% of the cost or whatever you feel is appropriate based on the level of service.

TOILETS

Public toilets can be found at many marinas and in shopping centers, such as the International Bazaar and Port Lucaya Marketplace on Grand Bahama. In the Out Islands, ask at bars or restaurants, as public facilities are practically nonexistent.

TOURIST INFORMATION

For general information before you go contact the **Bahamas Tourist Office** at one of the following locations:

Canada: 121 Bloor Street East, Suite 1101, Toronto, Ontario M4W 3M5; Tel. (416) 968-2999; fax (416) 968-6711.

UK: 3 The Billings, Walnut Tree Close, Guilford, Surrey, GU1 4UL; Tel. (01483) 448-900; fax (01483) 448-990.

US: 8600 West Bryn Mawr Avenue, Suite 820, Chicago, IL 60631; Tel. (773) 693-1500; fax (773) 693-1114.

World Trade Center, Suite 116, 2050 Stemmons Freeway, P.O. Box 581408, Dallas, TX 75258-1408; Tel. (214) 742-1886; fax (214) 741-4118.

3450 Wilshire Boulevard, Suite 1204, Los Angeles, CA 90010; Tel. (213) 385-0033; fax (213) 383-3966.

One Turnberry Place, 19495 Biscayne Boulevard, 8th Floor, Aventura, FL 33180; Tel. (305) 932-0051; fax (305) 682-8758.

150 East 52nd Street, 28th Floor North, New York, NY 10022; Tel. (212) 578-2777; fax (212) 753-6531.

Several of the islands have tourist bureaus of their own:

Nassau/New Providence: P.O. Box N-3701, Market Plaza, Bay Street, Nassau; Tel. 322-7501.

Grand Bahama Island Tourism Board: P.O. Box F 40251, Freeport, Grand Bahama Island; Tel. (242) 352-8356; fax (242) 352-2714 or 352-7840.
1 Turnberry Place, 19495 Biscayne Boulevard, Suite #809, Aventura, FL 33180; Tel. 800-448-3386 or (305) 935-9461; fax (305) 935-9464; website <www.interknowledge.com/bahamas>.

The Out Island Promotion Board: In US and Canada; Tel. 800-688-7452 or (954) 359- 8099; fax (954) 359-8098.

For tourist information once you have arrived in the Bahamas, contact the Ministry of Tourism at one or more of the following offices:

Nassau/New Providence: P.O. Box N-3701, Market Plaza, Bay Street, Nassau; Tel. 322-7501.
    Bay Street, Nassau; Tel. 356-7591.
    Nassau International Airport; Tel. 377-6806.

Grand Bahama Island: P.O. Box F40251, International Bazaar; Tel. 352-8044.
    Freeport International Airport; Tel. 352-2052.
    Port Lucaya Marketplace; Tel. 373-8988.

Abaco: P.O. Box AB-20663, Dove Plaza, Marsh Harbour; Tel. 367-3067.

Bimini: Alice Town; Tel. 347-3529.

Eleuthera: Bay Street, Dunmore Town, Harbour Island; Tel. 333-2621; fax 332-2622.
  Sunset House, Queens Highway, Governor's Harbour; Tel. 332-2142; fax 332-2480.

Exumas: Cousins Building, Queens Highway, George Town; Tel. 336-2430.

WEIGHTS and MEASURES

The Bahamas use US measurement systems.

Length

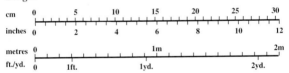

Weight

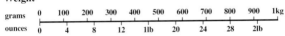

Temperature

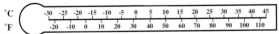

YOUTH HOSTELS

There are no youth hostels in the Bahamas.

Recommended Hotels

There is a wide choice of accommodation in the Bahamas, both in terms of style and price. At the upper end of the scale are very expensive but luxurious resort hotels with a comprehensive range of facilities such as shopping malls and golf courses. More modest accommodation can be found in small guest-houses and family-run hotels in Nassau. Some historic houses have been converted into hotels offering a "colonial feel," and these are complimented by modern, purpose built "all-inclusive" resorts, where use of every facility in the hotel is included in the price. Many hotels welcome children and have special programs for them but others operate an "adults only" policy. There are very few lodgings in the budget category.

The following selection of hotels covers a range of accommodation options. The price ranges quoted are in US dollars for double occupancy and for room only, except for the "all inclusive" hotels (indicated by AI), whose rates include all meals, drinks, and sports facilities. Many hotels add service charge of 15% to prices; resorts add a tax of 4%–6% . Prices can vary enormously between high and low season, with winter (Nov–Feb) generally being the most expensive.

✹✹✹✹✹	above $300
✹✹✹✹	$220–$300
✹✹✹	$150–$220
✹✹	$100–$150
✹	below $100

NEW PROVIDENCE

Nassau

Compass Point ✹✹✹✹ *PO Box CB-13842, West Bay St.; Tel. 327-4500 or 800-OUTPOST; fax 327-3299; website <www.islandlife.com>*. Very colorful wooden cottage-style rooms amid palm trees on about ½ hectare (1½ acres) of land near a small beach and jetty. Some of the elevated cottages have fully equipped kitchens and open-air dining areas beneath. Ceiling fans and netted, slatted windows offer a tropical feel. Small pool. 20 rooms. Major credit cards.

Graycliff ✪✪✪✪✪ *PO Box N 10246, West Hill St.; Tel. 322-2796/7; fax 326-6110.* Built over 250 years ago, this historic mansion has seen the likes of Winston Churchill and the Duke of Windsor. Some of the rooms have balconies, and all are air-conditioned and have large *en-suite* shower baths. Large Olympic-size swimming pool. Continental breakfast is included. The hotel's five-star restaurant serves continental and Bahamian cuisine and stocks one of the Caribbean's largest wine cellars. 14 rooms. Major credit cards.

Nassau Marriott Resort & Crystal Palace Casino ✪✪✪✪ *PO Box N-8306; Tel. 327-6200 or 800-228-9290; fax 327-4346.* Pastel purples and pinks dominate in the conservatively elegant interior; all rooms have either atrium or beach views and include *en-suite* spa shower baths. Tropical pool and lagoon area, swimming pool with water slide and sunken swim-up bar, and ½ mile of safe beach with palm trees and water sports facilities. Wheelchair access to some rooms. Twelve restaurants. 867 Rooms. Major credit cards.

Orange Hill Beach Inn ✪✪ *PO Box N-8583; Tel. 327-7157; fax 327-5186; e-mail <orangehill@batelnet.bs>; website <www.orangehill.com>.* On a hilltop overlooking the ocean (just a two-minute walk away), this unpretentious, friendly hotel has a laid-back, casual ambience. A mixture of rooms, studios, and apartments, all with *en-suite* shower baths, air-conditioning, and ceiling fans. Laundry facilities on-site. Five minutes from Cable Beach and 15 minutes from Nassau town by bus or taxi. Tours and scuba diving expeditions can be arranged through the hotel. Small restaurant. 32 rooms. Major credit cards.

Radisson Cable Beach Resort ✪✪✪-✪✪✪✪ *Bay St.; Tel. 237-6000 or (305) 932-0222; fax 237-6987 or (305) 932-0023;*

e-mail <radcblebch@aol.com>, website <www.radisson.com>. This resort is based around the golf club, although tennis, squash, and gym facilities are also available along with the usual beach activities on the property's 1000-ft (305-m) beachfront. Three large landscaped pools with waterfalls, cascade and misting pools, and a swim-up bar. Reservations required at all the restaurants except the buffet. 691 rooms. Major credit cards.

Sandals Royal Bahamian Resort & Spa ✪✪✪✪✪ (AI) *PO Box CB 13005, West Bay St.; tel. 327-6400/2 or 800–SANDALS; fax 327-6961; website <www.sandals.com>*. On Cable Beach just 15 minutes from downtown Nassau, this luxurious hotel combines the splendors of ancient Rome with the classical opulence of Versailles. Two large fresh-water pools, several misting whirlpools and mini-pools, and an award-winning spa. Excellent complimentary water-sport facilities on-site or on Sandals Cay ½-mile offshore. Six restaurants. 410 rooms. Major credit cards.

Paradise Island

Atlantis ✪✪✪-✪✪✪✪✪ *Box N 4777; Tel. 363-3000, (954) 713-2500, or 800-722-7466; fax 363-3957, (954) 713-2098, or 800-232-9748; website <www.sunint.com/atlantis/index.html>*. This huge structure takes up one end of the northern beach of Paradise Island. Not so much a hotel as a total holiday experience, with man-made beaches and shallow pools providing the opportunity to wade and swim with tropical fish. Clear underwater tube walkways bring you face to face with rays, hammerhead sharks, and other creatures. In the main lobby, the Great Hall of Waters, seven ornate columns support a cupola of Greek-style mosaic murals. Large casino complex. Outside is a 63-slip marina for vessels ranging from 40 ft to 220 ft (12 m to 67 m). 2,300 rooms. Major credit cards.

Bay View Village ✪✪-✪✪✪ *PO Box SS-6308; Tel. 363-2555 or 800-757-1357; fax 363-2370; e-mail <bayview@batelnet.bs>; website <www.bayviewvillage.com>*. A collection of one-, two-, and three-bedroom villas set in a tranquil atmosphere with gardens stocked with fruit trees and shrubs, just 5 minutes from Cabbage Beach. All villas have fully equipped kitchens and air-conditioning and ceiling fans. Three communal swimming pools and two villas with private pools. Centrally located laundry facilities. Tennis court, and tennis pro for lessons. The grounds and lower units are wheelchair accessible. 33 rooms. Major credit cards.

Ocean Club ✼✼✼✼✼ *PO Box N-4777; Tel. 363-3000; fax 363-2424; website <www.lhw.com/paradise/oceanclub.html>.* Relaxed luxury in a two-story colonial-style building; balconies overlook an Italianate courtyard with pool. The communal rooms were once the home of Huntingdon Hartford, owner of Paradise Island. All of the beautifully furnished guest rooms have air-conditioning and ceiling fans. A second pool adjoins a restaurant/café set in formal gardens with views towards The Cloisters. A beach bar/restaurant with wooden decking fronts on Cabbage Beach. 54 rooms. Major credit cards.

GRAND BAHAMA

Bahama Princess Resort and Casino ✼✼✼-✼✼✼✼ *PO Box F-40207, Freeport; Tel. 352-0661 or 800-223-1818; fax 352-7142.* Essentially two locations grouped as one hotel: both the casino side and the golf club side have well-appointed rooms with *en-suite* baths. Refrigerators and cribs are available for the rooms at no extra charge. Twelve tennis courts around a rock-sculptured pool with a waterfall and hot tub. Daily complimentary shuttle to Xanadu Beach. Sunken swim-up pool bar and nine restaurants. 965 rooms. Major credit cards.

Port Lucaya Yacht Club and Marina ✼✼✼ *Bell Channel Bay Road, PO Box F-42452, Freeport; Tel. 373-6618 or 800-LUCAYA-1; fax 373-6652; e-mail <vacation@batelnet.bs>; website <www.portlucaya.com/resort>.* A two-story resort just a minute's walk from Port Lucaya Market Place. The circular layout conceals interior gardens and a swimming pool area. Lower rooms face the garden; upper rooms look out over the waterways and port. All rooms have rattan furniture and terra cotta–tile floors. Laundry facilities. Transportation to nearby golf course. 160 rooms. Major credit cards.

Xanadu Beach Resort and Marina ✿✿✿ *Sunken Treasure Dr., PO Box F-402438, Freeport; Tel. 352-6782; fax (242) 352-5799.* Twelve-story high-rise hotel (the top floor was once home to Howard Hughes). A short walk through the beach bar and restaurant and marketplace selling Bahamian goods leads to a wide, gently shelving beach protected by breakwaters. Children's nursery available during the day (except Sunday). Two tennis courts by the side of a 44-slip marina. 286 rooms. Major credit cards.

THE ABACOS

Elbow Cay

Hope Town Hideaways ✿✿-✿✿✿ *Hope Town, Abaco; Tel. 366-1224; fax 366-1434; e-mail <peg@hopetown.com>; website <www.hopetown.com>.* Set in lush gardens on the lighthouse end of Hope Town. Pretty family-sized cottages with fully fitted kitchens accommodate 4 to 6 people. Swimming pool and laundry facilities. A small boat is provided with each rental so guests can get around the harbor. The proprietors also act as agents for the rental of private houses. 4 cottages. Major credit cards.

Great Guana Cay

Dolphin Club Resort and Marina ✿✿✿-✿✿✿✿ *Great Guana Cay, Abaco; Tel. 365 5137.* Colorful free-standing cottages and a lodge house along 800 feet (244 m) of pristine beach protected by sand dunes. Cottages have fully equipped kitchens and such unusual features as swinging queen-size beds and loft rooms with splendid views of the sea and harbor. Unfinished wooden walls painted in bright colors are complemented by funky cushions, hammocks, and bedding. All rooms have air-conditioning, ceiling fans, and *en-suite* showers; terraces and verandas offer tropical views in all directions. 8 rooms. Major credit cards.

Green Turtle Cay

Bluff House ✿✿✿ *Green Turtle Cay, Abaco; Tel. 365-4247; fax 365-4248; e-mail <bluffhouse.oii.net>; website <www.peaceandplenty.com> or <www.bluffhouse.com>.* Located on a bluff that affords excellent views of the sunrise over the Atlantic Ocean and the sunset over the Sea of Abaco. Split-level suites, villas, and one- and two-bedroom air-conditioned rooms, just steps from the water's edge, are all connected by a boardwalk—you feel as if you're wandering through a tropical forest. 25 rooms. Major credit cards.

Green Turtle Club and Marina ✿✿✿-✿✿✿✿ *Green Turtle Cay, Abaco; Tel. 365-4271; fax 365-4272; e-mail <greenturtle@batelnet.bs>; website <www.greenturtleclub.com>.* At the head of a tranquil crystal-clear harbor that shelters some of the world's finest yachts. All rooms are decorated with elegant Queen Anne mahogany furniture and are equipped with air conditioning and ceiling fans and refrigerators. Some rooms front the dockside; others surround the fresh-water lap pool. 37 rooms. Major credit cards.

Marsh Harbour

Abaco Beach Resort and Boat Harbour ✿✿✿-✿✿✿✿ *PO Box AB-20511, Marsh Harbour, Abaco; Tel. 367-2158; fax 367-2819.* Spacious rooms and villas set in 56 acres (23 hectares) alongside a large marina. Ten minutes from the airport and five minutes from ferry terminal to central Abaco Cays. Water sports and diving center on-site. 52 rooms, 6 villas. Major credit cards.

Treasure Cay

Treasure Cay Hotel Resort and Marina ✿✿✿-✿✿✿✿ *Treasure Cay Services, 2301 South Federal Highway, Fort Lauderdale, Florida 33316; Tel. (954) 525-7711; fax (954) 525-1699; e-mail <info@treasurecay.com>; website <www.treasurecay.com>.* Set around the Treasure Cay marina, only a few minutes' walk from the five-mile beach. 18-hole golf course. Boat rental and diving and snorkeling outings can be arranged at extra cost. Rooms have bay or harbor views. 96 rooms. Major credit cards.

SAN SALVADOR

Riding Rock Inn ✿✿-✿✿✿ *Cockburn Town; Tel. 331-2631 or (954) 359-8353; fax 331-2020 or (954) 359-8254; e-mail <ridingrock@aol.com>; website <www.ridingrock.com>.* Located on a deserted white-sand beach at the edge, 1,640 ft (500 m) off the end of the runway. The atmospheric Driftwood Bar is decorated with seafaring memorabilia; every available free space—walls, tabletops, ceilings, doors—is covered with imaginative notes from former guests, on business cards, pieces of driftwood, even strips of T-shirts and old hats. Well-appointed rooms, tiled throughout, have views of the sea or the pool. Refrigerators provided in the deluxe rooms. Excellent dive facility close by. 42 rooms. Major credit cards.

ELEUTHERA

Coral Sands Hotel ✿✿✿ *Harbour Island, Eleuthera; Tel. 333-2320; fax 333-2368; e-mail <reservations@coralsands.com>; website <www.coralsands.com>.* Situated on the island's famous pink sand beach, this hotel has a relaxed yet elegant feel. Small, pretty rooms have coffee facilities and refrigerators. Two restaurants—one on a deck near the beach for daytime and a fine dining room with excellent food and wine list, for evening. Water sports equipment available. 27 rooms. Major credit cards.

The Cove ✿✿ *PO Box 1548, Gregory Town, Eleuthera; Tel. 335-5142; fax 332-2691; e-mail <thecove@batelnet.com>; website <www.thecoveeleuthera.com>.* A basic, no-frills accommodation on a sheltered beach. A range of sports equipment, including bicycles and snorkel gear, is included in the room rental and the owners are a mine of information about Eleuthera. Swimming pool. Restaurant. 26 rooms. Major credit cards.

Pink Sands ✿✿✿✿✿ *Harbour Island, Eleuthera; Tel. 333-2030; fax 333-2060; e-mail <outpost800@aol.com>; website*

<www.islandlife.com>. Situated on 16 acres fronting a beautiful pink-sand beach sheltered by a barrier reef. All rooms have air-conditioning and ceiling fans, walk-in wardrobes, and private out-side patios with teak furniture. Rough-cut Italian marble floors are covered with area rugs; the walls sport a mellow wash of pink and blue. The facilities include 3 tennis courts, one lit for night play, a freshwater pool, fitness gym, gift shop, and a beach restaurant and bar. Prices include evening meal. 26 rooms. Major credit cards.

THE EXUMAS

Great Exuma Island

Club Peace and Plenty ✸✸ *PO Box 29055, George Town, Exuma; Tel. (809) 336-2551 or 800-525-2210; fax (809) 336-2093; e-mail <ssbpeace@aol.com>; website <www.peaceandplenty.com>*. A coral-pink, colonial, waterfront hotel surrounded by palm trees and overlooking the boardwalk and moorings of Bonefish Bay. Although there is no beach, the hotel provides boat service to Stocking Island, which has excellent beaches. All the guest rooms have either a terrace or balcony. Small pool. In-door/outdoor restaurant. 35 rooms. Major credit cards.

Coconut Cove ✸✸ *PO Box EX 29299, George Town, Exuma; Tel. 336-2659; fax 336-2658*. This colonial-style clapboard hotel offers a mix of beach-front and garden-front rooms, all with queen-size beds, air-conditioning, and *en-suite* baths. Private ter-races with garden furniture offer views of the lush garden oasis with palms and a salt-water pond stocked with fish. Compact fresh-water pool, beach bar, and a small sandy beach with board-walk looking out to Stocking Island. 10 rooms. Major credit cards.

Regatta Point ✸✸-✸✸✸ *PO Box 6, George Town, Exuma; Tel. 336-2206 or 800-668-0389; fax 336-2046*. A colonial-style house on a pretty Casaurina tree–lined point in the waters of Elizabeth Harbour. This tranquil setting provides distance from the bustle of George Town yet it's close enough to stroll into town for supplies. All wood-paneled rooms have fully equipped kitchens with all amenities. Air-conditioning fans in the high ceilings and mosquito nets. Patios and terraces offer views across the bay. 6 rooms. Major credit cards.

Stocking Island

Hotel Higgins Landing ❋❋❋ *PO Box EX 29146, George Town, Exuma; Tel 336-2460; fax 357-0008; e-mail <stockisl@aol.com>; website <www.higginslanding.com>.* An award-winning, eco-friendly colonial-style hotel set on a beautiful white-sand beach and lagoon. The entire facility is 100% solar-powered, with wind-power backup; no water is pulled from the ground and only natural resources are used. The cottages are decorated with antiques and all rooms have queen-size beds, tiled showers and floors, ceiling fans, screened windows, and private decks. Dining is an occasion here (reservations required by noon): dinner is served in a romantic candle-lit dining room straight out of a Caribbean plantation great house. The shallow cove is ideal for snorkeling, kayaking, or sailing (complimentary equipment provided). 5 rooms. Major credit cards.

ANDROS

Andros Island Bone Fishing Lodge ❋❋❋❋ *Cargill Creek, Andros; Tel. 368-5167; fax 368-5235.* Clapboard cabins in the heart of prime fishing country, with flats right outside the door. Rates include accommodation, meals, and a full program of fishing. There is little to do onshore, so this place is definitely for committed anglers. 8 cabins. MasterCard, Visa (with 5% surcharge).

Small Hope Bay Lodge ❋❋❋ *AI PO Box 21667, Ft. Lauderdale, FL 33335-1667 or PO Box CB 11817, Nassau; Tel. 368-2013/4 or 800-223-6961; fax 368-2015; e-mail <shbinfo@smallhope.com>; website <www.smallhope.com>.* A friendly and laid-back family-run lodge on a pristine natural beach that stretches for 15 miles (9 km). Guest rooms are decorated with Andros pine, coral-stone walls, ceiling fans, and Androsia batik soft furnishings. A major fishing and dive center (inclusive packages available). 20 rooms. Major credit cards.

Recommended Restaurants

The Bahamas are blessed with a wealth of restaurants that serve both local specialties and international cuisine. Most of the larger resort hotels on New Providence and Grand Bahama have acclaimed dining rooms that are open to the public, but there are also many independent establishments with a high reputation and a faithful clientele. On the Out Islands, the choice and range is more limited but the standards are still high.

In the high season it's best to always make a reservation. Out-of-season reservations are appreciated at all times but should definitely been made on the weekends. Some of the more expensive establishments have a dress code.

If calling to make a reservation from outside the Bahamas first dial the area code, 242.

The following price guidelines are for the cost of a three-course dinner, per person, without drinks, tax, or tips. Prices are in US dollars.

✿✿✿✿✿	above $100
✿✿✿✿	$60–$100
✿✿✿	$40–$60
✿✿	$25–$40
✿	below $25

NEW PROVIDENCE

Cable Beach

Black Angus Grill ✿✿✿-✿✿✿✿ *Nassau Marriott Resort and Crystal Palace Casino; Tel. 327-6200.* Gourmet steaks, lamb, and seafood served in an elegant environment. Jacket required. Reservations preferred. Open for dinner daily 6pm–11pm. Major credit cards.

Bahamas

Café Johnny Canoe ✿✿-✿✿✿ *Nassau Beach Hotel; Tel. 327-3373.* American and Bahamian dishes such as prime rib, burgers, grouper fillet, and cracked conch served inside, or outside on the patio. Casual. Open daily 7:30am–12am. Entertainment Thursday to Saturday, nights. Major credit cards.

Capriccio Ristorante ✿✿-✿✿✿ *West Bay St.; Tel. 327-8547.* In the heart of Cable Beach, this restaurant offers authentic Italian cuisine, accompanied by violin music. The menu includes a wide variety of pastas along with beef, chicken, and seafood dishes. Open Monday to Saturday 11am–10pm. Major credit cards.

Sea Shells ✿✿-✿✿✿ *Crystal Cay Marina Park, West Bay St., off Arawak Cay; Tel. 328-1036.* A casually elegant seafood restaurant, though it also serves Angus beef. Specialties include Cajun dishes and Bahamian favorite. Wonderful ocean views. Open Monday to Saturday 11am–3pm, 6pm–11pm. Major credit cards.

Paradise Island

Anthony's Caribbean Grill ✿✿ *Paradise Island Shopping Plaza; Tel. 363-3152.* Caribbean/American no-frills restaurant with good-quality food. Sports-bar environment with TV sets and music. Open daily 11:30am–11pm. Major credit cards.

Columbus Tavern ✿✿✿-✿✿✿✿ *Paradise Harbour Club and Marina, Paradise Island Dr.; Tel. 363-2534.* From the dining room you can watch the yachts in Nassau Harbour. Steak Diane and Lobster Flambé are the standout signature dishes on the fine menu. Reservations recommended for lunch and dinner. Open daily 7am–10:30pm. Major credit cards.

Nassau

Buena Vista ✺✺✺-✺✺✺✺ *West Hill St. and Delancy St.; Tel. 322-2811/2.* Established in 1946, this acclaimed restaurant in a 19th-century house offers an extensive selection of Continental and Bahamian specialties along with a choice of 150 wines. Jackets for men are suggested attire. Open for dinner Monday–Saturday from 7pm. Reservations recommended. Major credit cards.

Café Matisse ✺✺ *Bank Lane and Bay St., off Parliament Square; Tel. 356-7012.* The walls of this picturesque restaurant are covered with prints of works by Matisse. Courtyard dining for outdoor meals. Pasta, pizza, and seafood dominate the menu. Open Monday to Saturday 10am–11pm. Major credit cards.

The Cellar ✺✺-✺✺✺ *11 Charlotte St.; Tel. 322-8877.* Late 18th-century house and patio with wooden floorboards create an "olde worlde" atmosphere. Special dishes include quiche, salad, and pasta along with Bahamian and English favorites. Open for lunch Monday–Saturday 11am–4pm. Major credit cards.

Crocodiles Waterfront Bar and Grill ✺✺ *East Bay St.; Tel. 323-3341.* This funky island-style bar and grill on the harbor front defines casual Bahamian dining: enjoy Caribbean and American favorites while relaxing outside under thatched "tiki" huts. Open daily 11am–12am. Major credit cards.

Graycliff ✺✺✺✺-✺✺✺✺✺ *West Hill St.; Tel. 322-2797.* Elegant restaurant in a 250-year-old Colonial mansion. Offering the best of gourmet food, this is the only 5-star restaurant in the Bahamas. Award-winning wine cellar. Reservations requested. Open for lunch Monday to Friday 12–3pm. Dinner daily 7–10pm. Major credit cards.

The Poop Deck ✺✺-✺✺✺ *East Bay St., Nassau Yacht Haven Marina; Tel. 393-8175.* A casual, tropical restaurant set right in the heart of Nassau Harbour. Bahamian and American dishes. Open daily 12–10:30pm. Major credit cards.

GRAND BAHAMA

Arawak Dining Room ✹✹✹ *Lucayan Country Golf Club, Freeport-Lucaya; Tel. 373-1066.* A spacious elegant restaurant offering French cuisine with a Bahamian accent. Open daily 11am–3pm, 6:30–10pm. Live jazz music in the evenings. Major credit cards.

Banana Bay Restaurant and Bar ✹✹ *Fortune Beach, Lucaya. Tel. 373-2960.* Dine in the colorfully painted clapboard interior, or out on a wooden deck. Conch fritters and conch salad are among the Bahamian dishes on offer alongside burgers and sandwiches. Very casual. Open Monday to Saturday 9am–5:30pm, Sunday 10am–5:30pm. MasterCard, Visa.

Ferry House Restaurant ✹✹✹ *Pelican Bay, Port Lucaya; Tel. 373-1595.* Located by the ferry stop in Pelican Bay, this quaint restaurant with pretty table linens and woven straw chairs serves fine Danish and Continental cuisine. Outdoor seating is available on a small deck area. Weekly barbecue. Major credit cards.

Luciano's ✹✹✹✹ *Port Lucaya; Tel. 373-9100.* Gourmet Continental cuisine in an elegant setting. Upstairs on the dock front overlooking the marina. Open Monday to Saturday from 6pm. Reservations recommended. Major credit cards.

Pier One Restaurant ✹✹✹ *Freeport Harbour, Tel 352-6674.* Perched at the end of a jetty along the entrance to Freeport harbor, this restaurant, renowned for its seafood, offers fine views of the commercial and cruise vessels entering and departing. Seating for 250. Try to time your meal for the daily shark-feeding event: each evening free ocean sharks swim into the rocky area beneath the decks for their snack. Open Monday to Saturday 10am–10pm, Sunday 3–10pm. Major credit cards.

Ruby Swiss ✪✪✪✪ *West Sunrise Highway and Atlantic Way, Freeport; Tel. 352-8507.* A fine Bahamian restaurant with a touch of Europe. One of the most popular places on the island. Extensive wine list. Live entertainment nightly. Open daily from 11am; dinner from 6pm. Major credit cards.

Shenanigans ✪✪✪ *Port Lucaya Marketplace; Tel. 373-4734.* Traditional Irish Pub with good hearty food, including Irish stew. Selection of international beers on tap. Open Monday to Saturday noon–midnight. Major credit cards.

THE OUT ISLANDS

The Abacos

Cap'n Jacks Restaurant and **Bar** ✪✪ *Harbour Front, Hope Town, Elbow Cay, Abaco; Tel. 366-0247.* A casual bar and restaurant at the harbor's edge serving American and Bahamian food. Live music twice weekly. Sports TV on satellite. Call for hours of operation. Major credit cards.

Green Turtle Club and Marina ✪✪✪-✪✪✪✪ *Green Turtle Cay, Abaco; Tel. 365-4271, fax 365-4272.* Lounge on elegant mahogany Queen Anne furniture inside or, in the summer, enjoy the breezes in the outdoor dining area. American and Continental cuisine. Call for hours of operation. Major credit cards.

Harbour's Edge ✪✪ *Harbour Front, Hope Town, Elbow Cay, Abaco; Tel. 366-0087/0292.* A popular gathering spot—locals come here for grilled fish and conch specialties. Open 11am–3pm, 6–9pm. Closed Tuesday. MasterCard, Visa.

Sapodilly's ✪✪-✪✪✪ *Bay St., Marsh Harbour; Tel. 367-3498.* This casual spot serves local specialties, including fresh fish, pork, and conch served "any which way." Harbor and sunset views. Live music Thursday, Friday, and Saturday. Open daily 11:30am–3pm, 6:30–9pm. Major credit cards.

The Tipsy Seagull ❀❀ *Treasure Cay Resort, Treasure Cay; Tel. 365-8469.* Open-air bar where everyone gathers to watch the sunset. Barbecue, pizza, and regular buffets. Friday night junkanoo celebrations. Call for hours. Major credit cards.

Wally's Restaurant ❀❀❀ *Bay St., Marsh Harbour; Tel. 363-2074.* Situated in an old Abaco home, this elegant dining room presents an array of Bahamian, American, and Continental dishes. Open daily 11:30am–3pm, 6–9pm. Live music Wednesday and Saturday evenings. Major credit cards.

Eleuthera

Poseidon Restaurant ❀❀❀ *Coral Sands Hotel, Harbour Island; Tel. 333-2320, fax 333-2368.* Relaxed yet elegant restaurant serving excellent classical French cuisine. Well-chosen wine list. Open for dinner daily 7–9pm. Major credit cards.

The Exumas

Hotel Higgins Landing ❀❀❀❀ *PO Box EX 29146, George Town, Exuma; Tel. 336-2460, fax 357-0008.* A small, romantic candle-lit restaurant in an eco-friendly hotel. The set menu, which changes daily, is based around fresh local ingredients. Cocktails at 6:30pm and dinner at 7pm. Reservations must be placed by noon. Boat transfer is available to and from George Town or to and from your boat. Major credit cards.

Bimini

Fisherman's Wharf ❀❀❀ *King's Highway, Alice Town; Tel. 347-3371.* Many say it's the best food in the Bimini Islands: seafood and Bahamian favorites. Open daily noon–10pm. Major credit cards.